GRAND OLD GAME: 365 DAYS OF BASEBALL

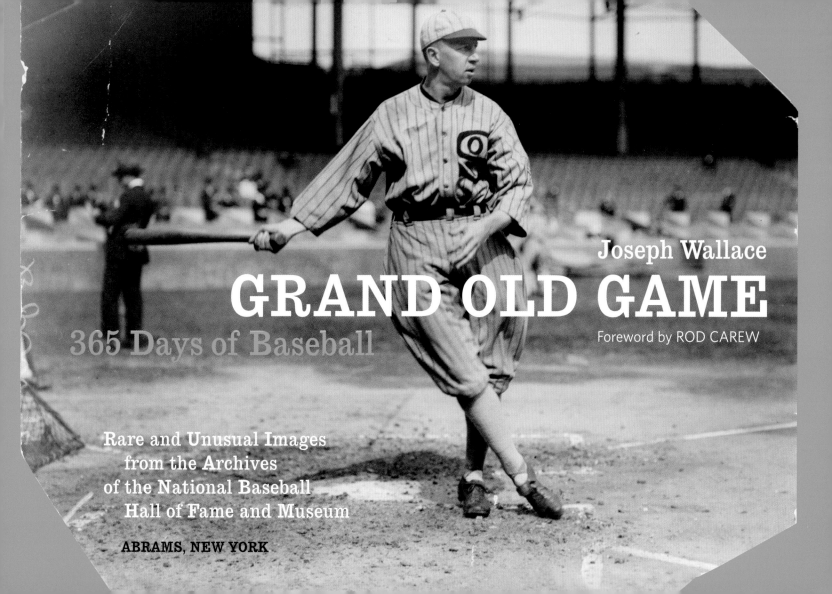

Joseph Wallace

GRAND OLD GAME

Foreword by ROD CAREW

365 Days of Baseball

Rare and Unusual Images
from the Archives
of the National Baseball
Hall of Fame and Museum

ABRAMS, NEW YORK

MY PASSION for baseball began when I was a small boy in Panama taking every opportunity to swing a broom handle at anything that resembled a ball. When I wasn't playing, my ears were always glued to whatever scratchy game play-by-play broadcast I could pick up on Armed Forces Radio.

My passion for photography began when I received my first camera as a gift from Sy Berger of the Topps Baseball Card Company. I particularly enjoyed my newfound ability to record life from a different perspective.

As my baseball career progressed, I would use my photography as a getaway from the daily grind of a 162-game schedule. I was never without my camera on the road, stealing away to the quiet docks in the port of Seattle to shoot the workers, or just walking the streets of New York, Chicago, or Boston looking for distinctive faces that hid a lifetime of secrets.

At home, especially during my years with the Angels, my tripod and cameras were always set up at the end of the dugout ready to peek into the eyes of Gene Mauch or record the amazing raw power of the likes of Reggie Jackson, Don Baylor, and Nolan Ryan.

During these years I also grew to know and respect the guys in the camera wells for the terrific job they do in capturing our great game. The late V. J. Lovero was a particular favorite of mine. Without him and others like him, so many baseball memories would be lost.

So it is with great pleasure that I write the foreword to *Grand Old Game: 365 Days of Baseball*. More than any other game, baseball is steeped in history, and this rich history lives on in the pages of this wonderful book.

—Rod Carew

EVER SINCE I was a child, I've been an enthusiastic collector of things. Coins, base-ball cards, bottlecaps. Lost golf balls at the course near the house where I spent summer vacations. The names of the birds that came through my backyard in Brooklyn. And, to my mom's horror, endless bugs, salamanders, and snakes.

It was never the *having* that excited me the most, but the search, the hunt. In each case, what I remember most clearly is the surprise and pleasure I felt when I came upon my latest prize. Finding that elusive Cleon Jones card, dusty from the stick of fossilized gum they used to put in the Topps pack. Turning over a log to reveal a tiny, perfect garter snake. Discovering eleven lost golf balls on a single day: five in the underbrush beyond the sixth hole, five more in a water trap on seventeen, and one impaled on a sharp branch fifty feet off the first fairway.

My collections are long gone, but I'm still lucky enough to have the chance to exper-ience the pleasures of hunting for treasure. Today I search for good stories to use in the books I write, facts about baseball and other subjects that will make readers laugh or shake their heads or think about things in a slightly different way. When I come upon a detail new to me in an old newspaper, long-out-of-print book, or conversation, I get the same quiet thrill I felt when I found a newt or a Nolan Ryan rookie card.

But no previous treasure hunt compares to the one that led to the book you're holding. For this quest took me to the National Baseball Hall of Fame Library—specifically, to its magnificent collection of photographs, currently numbering more than 400,000.

Where to begin when facing such a wealth of treasure? Of course I checked out the files on Babe Ruth, Ted Williams, Ty Cobb, and Lou Gehrig, among the most photographed ballplayers of all time. But instead of focusing on the most famous, most widely published images, I searched for the strangest, funniest, most revealing ones I could find. And, as in all successful treasure hunts, I struck paydirt.

Many of my favorites show players off the field. Here is the grinning young Ruth playing football; the ever-intense Cobb huddled over a checkerboard; Gehrig reeling in a big one on a New Jersey fishing boat; Williams bravely eating a live clam while on military service in Korea. But I don't neglect their on-the-field activities: Cobb spiking his way into third; Ruth launching one; Gehrig looking like a Greek god even in batting practice; Williams demonstrating his flawless swing.

Nor have I left out a myriad of others who have helped make baseball the greatest game on earth. Willie Mays uncorking one of his typically astounding throws. Jackie Robinson at the plate, all of his aggressiveness and skill channeled into his battle with the pitcher. Mickey Mantle, the essence of cool, sliding home. Josh Gibson and other Negro League immortals; the women of the All-American Professional Girls Baseball League; a gallery of feisty managers from John McGraw through Earl Weaver; fans, umpires, Little Leaguers, military ballplayers, and an assortment of visiting celebrities ranging from the Marx Brothers to Al Capone.

In many cases, I was able to find the fascinating stories behind the most surprising images. In other cases (what *were* the Washington Senators and Redskins doing on the same ballfield at the same time?) the background story has been lost to history. Or maybe not: If you have anything to tell me—and the Hall of Fame—about any of these pictures, let me know. You can contact me through my website, www.josephwallace.com. I hope to hear from you!

As I'm sure you can imagine, I had a wonderful time finding these images. I hope that paging through *Grand Old Game* will seem like a treasure hunt to you as well—and that the treasure will be worth the search. Happy hunting!

AS ALWAYS, and now more than ever, I am deeply grateful to my friends at the National Baseball Hall of Fame Library and Archive. With her smarts, good humor, and unparalleled knowledge of the collection, Pat Kelly was the guide of my dreams. Bill Burdick made this project possible (as well as taking on the challenge of scanning all the images), while Dale Petroskey, Scot Mondore, and Bill Haase helped transform it into an official Hall of Fame project—a development that I can still hardly believe.

At the Hall of Fame Library, Jim Gates insured that my text would be as accurate as possible by handing it on to a group of brilliant readers/baseball historians: Tim Wiles, Gabriel Schechter, Bill Francis, Russell Wolinsky, and Erik Strohl. (As always, blame the author for any errors that remain.) Tim Wiles deserves extra thanks for his warmth, thoughtfulness, and insights, which led me to some photographs I otherwise would never have found. Claudette Burke runs an incomparable research room, simultaneously friendly and efficient, while Freddy Berowski was always there to answer a question or lug up yet another photo file.

At Abrams, I am grateful to editor-in-chief Eric Himmel for giving me the chance to begin this treasure hunt and to my brilliant editor, Sharon AvRutick, and designer, Helene Silverman, for making this book read as well and look as good as it does.

THEY CAME BY TRAIN

Let the baseball year begin! The New York Highlanders (soon to become and already being informally referred to as the "Yankees") took the slow train through Georgia from their spring-training headquarters in Macon for a 1909 exhibition game in Gray, the county seat. "The game was played on what was a cotton field not long ago," reported the *New York Times*. "The fielders looked into a clump of trees so that the batters had all the best of it, and both sides larruped the ball heartily."

THEY CAME BY RIVERBOAT

Before the era of transcontinental airplane travel, spring training was a chance to see parts of the country that seemed a world away. Here, in a 1919 photograph, the New York Giants make a stop in Florida. They must have been drenched in sweat in their heavy woolen suits, perfect for chilly northern springs but not for the steamy South. But early ballplayers, fighting the game's rowdy reputation, always dressed well off the field.

THEY CAME BY CAB

The 1913 Chicago White Sox pose in their road uniforms during a spring trip to Oakland, California, standing outside their "Acme Auto Taxicab." (Where are Roadrunner and Wile E. Coyote?) At the time, baseball was thought by many people to be "only one degree above grand larceny, arson, and mayhem," as Connie Mack put it, and players were often not welcome at a town's most respectable hotels.

CHICAGO WHITE SOX

"TEL OAKLAND", OAKLAND, CAL.
MARCH 6TH. TO 30TH. 1913

GAL. PHOTO Co.
509-16TH ST. OAK. CAL.

THEY CAME BY TROLLEY

In this undated photo likely taken in the late 1910s, Cleveland Indians players arrive in New Orleans for spring training. The life of a ballplayer in springtime was an itinerant one: Between 1900 and 1940, the Indians trained in Cleveland, New Orleans, San Antonio, Dallas, Atlanta, Macon, Mobile, Alexandria (Louisiana), Pensacola, Athens (Georgia), and Fort Myers and Lakeland (Florida).

THEY CAME BY...CAMEL?

One reason many players loathe spring training is the abundance of downtime to be filled. During their 1909 visit to Gray, Georgia, the New York Highlanders were diverted by a menagerie that included this unimpressed camel. The trip did have some other highlights: a party thrown by the local Women's Improvement Society, a barbecue hosted by the Gray Village Improvement Club (Gray was big on self-improvement), and the game itself, which raised money to build a local school.

ANYONE FOR SNOWBALL?

Pittsburgh Pirates pitchers and catchers huddle together for warmth on an early spring day in French Lick Springs, Indiana, circa 1912. Today, no team trains north of Florida or Arizona, but a century ago the expense and difficulty of travel often made teams try to economize by redefining "south" as any place much below New York, Cleveland, or Detroit— and then they sent players on train tours to places like French Lick Springs. Too often, the result was a snowy scene like this one.

INSPECTING THEIR BLUDGEONS

Three New York Giants (including Frank Frisch, left, and an uncharacteristically serious Casey Stengel, center) check out a new shipment of bats at spring training, circa 1923. "A well-tested bat is the batter's best friend," wrote scribe F. C. Lane in his 1925 book *Batting*. "For after all, mechanical ability and mental talents and experience must all express themselves by means of this inanimate bludgeon."

PYRAMID OF POWER

The high-spirited National League Champion Brooklyn Robins (formerly the Trolley Dodgers, eventually just the Dodgers) celebrate a new season at their Hot Springs, Arkansas, training camp in 1917. That's Hy Myers, Chief Meyers, and Ivy Olson on the bottom; Jim Hickman and Zack Wheat in the middle; and Jimmy Johnston on top. Unfortunately, the pyramid collapsed in 1917, as the Dodgers tumbled to a 70–81 record and a seventh-place finish.

HEY, CASEY!

Captain Frank Frisch (left) and other Giants teammates extend a warm welcome to Casey Stengel in spring training of 1922. Stengel joined the Giants in 1921, just in time to partake of a World Championship. Though Casey had a flair for dramatic feats—as witnessed by his two World Series home runs in 1923—he was never a great star, just (in the words of writer Frank Graham) "a lighthearted, freewheeling, old-time ball-player who, while never a dissipater, took his fun where he found it."

EAT YOUR VEGETABLES

A benefit of spring training: a supply of fresh fruit and veggies not easily available up in Pittsburgh. Touring through El Centro, California, in 1946, the Pirates and local officials chow down on carrots, cabbages, and "No-Needa Sugar" grapefruit before embarking on the trip back to San Bernardino, their spring training home.

THE WATCHER

No one else in baseball history looked anything like long, lanky, and gaunt Cornelius Alexander McGillicuddy, better known as Connie Mack. As manager of the Philadelphia Athletics from 1901 to 1950, he presided over two dynasties and more than his share of terrible teams. (His 1911 crew won 101 games and the World Series; five years later, the A's went 36-117.) But win or lose, Mack never lost his grave equilibrium. Here, he keeps an eye on Jimmie Foxx, the premier slugger of his 1929–31 dynasty.

ALL IN A DAY'S WORK

All-time great Honus Wagner (back row, third from left) and his Pittsburgh Pirates pose in front of their hotel in Hot Springs, Arkansas, in 1910. From that day to this, spring training has been a mix of short bursts of fun—barbecues, boat trips, the games themselves—and long stretches of tedium, including posing for team pictures. These players are not struggling to hide their ebullient enthusiasm.

AT THE BALLPARK

Eventually, baseball actually breaks out at spring training. In uniform are circa-1915 Philadelphia Phillies (left to right) Bill Killefer, Ed Burns, Joe Oeschger, George "Possum" Whitted, and Eppa Rixey, in St. Petersburg, Florida. They had plenty to smile about: The Phillies would win ninety games and the National League pennant in the upcoming season. Team leaders pitcher Grover Cleveland Alexander (thirty-one wins) and slugger Gavvy Cravath (twenty-four home runs) didn't bother to show up for the picture.

PAS DE THIRTY

Modern dance? No, calisthenics, as fitness coaches lead the St. Louis Cardinals through an agonizing ritual of spring training: getting into shape. No one had personal trainers back in those days, and most players had second jobs in the off-season. The spring was for sweating off a winter's worth of hamburgers and beer, and gradually getting your reflexes back. But it wasn't much fun.

THE OLD-TIMER AND THE ROOK

The man on the left is Chief Bender, who won 212 games in a Hall of Fame career with the Philadelphia Athletics and other teams (1903–17). In this shot from spring training in 1931, he's giving counsel to Harold Schumacher, "Prince Hal," a young rookie getting set for his first season in the bigs. Schumacher would go only 1–1 in 1931 and 5–6 in 1932, but in 1933 he would win nineteen games to help the Giants win the National League pennant. Add a victory in the Giants' five-game Series triumph over the Washington Senators, and you have a pretty big year for a prince who was still only twenty-two years old.

DOWN AND DIRTY

Even the stars had to hit the dirt in spring training when the New York Giants' John McGraw was their manager. Here the designated victim was Frank Frisch, the Fordham Flash, making the mud fly in 1923. "McGraw drove his men hard," wrote Bill James in his *New Historical Baseball Abstract*. "He pushed them to the breaking point." But McGraw's uncompromising ways paid off, both over the course of his long career and in 1923, when Frisch hit .348 and the Giants won the pennant.

THREE FEET AND A CLOUD OF DUST

New York Giants manager John McGraw circa 1921, supervising a baserunning drill during the Giants' spring season in San Antonio. And, yes, that's an actual grapefruit at McGraw's feet—perhaps to be used as a missile if one of the runners exhibited poor technique. Within a few years McGraw's dictatorial tactics would begin to wear out their welcome with the players, culminating in superstar Frank Frisch jumping the team in 1926.

Dirty Work *San Antonio, Texas Grafe 1926 Fan.*

DESERT FOX

Detroit Tigers manager Hughie Jennings keeps a close eye on an unidentified player—it looks as though it may be Ty Cobb—on a sandy, desolate practice field. (The man on the right is there to even out the dunes.) "It is hardest to get going in the early weeks of the race when the sliding sores are bad, but even then a player must hit the dirt as if he enjoyed it," said Cobb.

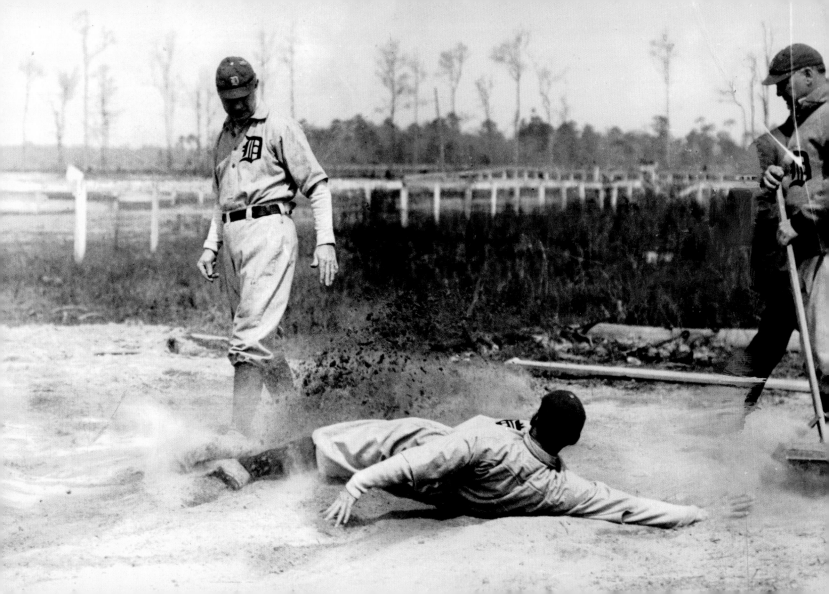

"HEY! LOOK AT ME!"

Spring training might be drudgery for veterans, but for rookies it's often the best chance to make an impression. Here are four New York Giants rookies—Hal Schumacher, Jim Mooney, Jim Tennant, and Sam Leslie— showing off what they've got in San Antonio in 1931. Unfortunately, the only observers seem to be a few moderately interested newspapermen.

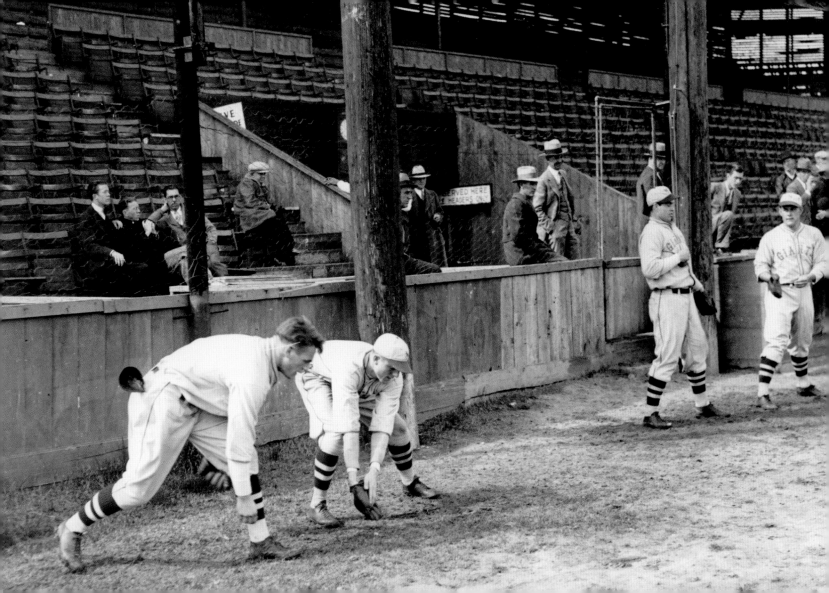

WORDS FROM A SAGE

Connie Mack (right) catches the attention of his latest generation of Philadelphia Athletics, in Mexico City in 1937—Mack's thirty-seventh year as A's manager. At this time, Mack was the only manager in the game who still wore a suit on the bench. "You're born with two strikes against you," he would tell players, "so don't take a third one on your own."

WALKING WOUNDED

Compared to football or hockey, baseball seems like a nonviolent game. But fans rarely see the sprains, strains, abrasions, and contusions that result from hard slides, quick turns, and bruising collisions with other players or the outfield wall—especially in spring training, when many players are out of shape and quickly end up in the trainer's room. "After the first two days of running in the spring sunshine, a ballplayer's feet look positively leprous, with blisters and lesions covering his aching toes and heels," reported Jim Brosnan in *The Long Season.*

IF AT FIRST

Lou Gehrig made everything look easy—but fielding at first base was an ongoing challenge for him. Before spring training began, he revealed, he would practice fielding ground balls on the floor of an indoor gymnasium. "The reason a wood floor is good, of course," he said, "is because the ball is easier to field. It bounds straight and true.... Learning to handle a ball indoors, therefore, gives a player confidence in his fielding ability." Confidence, it turns out, that Gehrig himself needed.

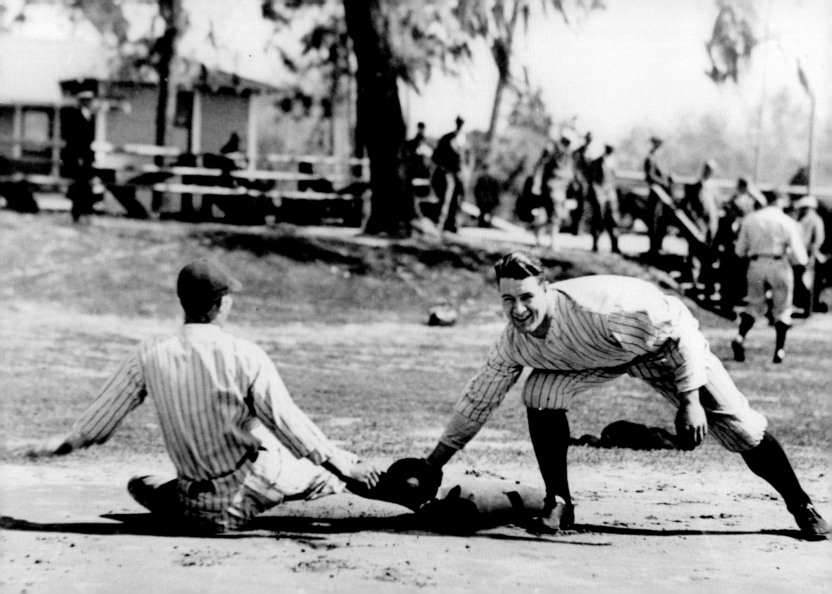

SPRING FASHIONS

On chill Texas mornings, the 1920 New York Giants wore what may have been the first "team coats"—overcoats more suited to a spy than a ball-player. The taller players were more successful at pulling off this daring fashion statement than were their shorter, dumpier teammates. And diminutive manager John McGraw (back row, center) looked like a plaid egg. Perhaps that's why the Giants soon abandoned this unusual garb.

THE BAD APPLE

The 1909 New York Highlanders seem peaceable in this spring-training photo. But there was trouble brewing. Star first baseman Hal Chase (back row, third from left) may have already been planning the ouster of manager George Stallings (center row, fourth from left). Though Stallings took a team that had lost 103 games in 1908 and made them a winner, rumors flew that Chase was losing games on purpose to sabotage the manager. Chase did, in fact, take over for Stallings in 1910, and the Highlanders went into a tailspin. The team didn't recover for a decade, by which time they had a new name, new ownership, and a right fielder named Babe Ruth.

A WHOLE NEW BALLGAME

Frank Frisch (left) and his World Champion New York Giants work over a medicine ball during spring training in 1923. Off-season and spring training exercise regimens were charmingly haphazard back then, especially when compared to the almost military intensity with which most players train today. For many players, winter exercise involved only hunting or fishing. Ty Cobb, for example, trekked through the Georgia woods after his hunting dogs—with lead inserts in his heavy boots to build up the muscles in his legs.

WHAT THE WELL-DRESSED MAN IS WEARING

The 1906 New York Giants lounge around the verandah of the St. Charles Hotel in New Orleans. Perhaps because of the bad reputation that ball-players then had among the general populace—they were considered crooked, lower-class drunks and bullies—off-the-field photos from the time often resemble this one. The players are almost always dressed in conservative, neatly creased suits and wear, or carry, snappy hats. The message, accurate or not, was, "We're not the rowdy roisterers you think we are! Come to the ballpark! Women and children welcome!"

EAGLE EYE

Manager John McGraw (in straw hat) keeps an eye on young Travis Jackson, the Giants' shortstop, during spring training in 1924. That must have been one tense spring: The Giants were coming off a shocking World Series loss to their loathed crosstown rivals, the Yankees. Nor was McGraw's mood improved by the Giants' spring quarters in Sarasota, Florida, where the team had to room in two separate hotels. As Frank Graham recalled in *The New York Giants*, "The hotels were separated by a long block and every night saw [McGraw] charging back and forth, making sure his athletes were observing the eleven o'clock curfew."

IF YOU BUILD IT....

A bird's-eye view of why the South was so popular for spring training: warm weather in late winter and as much flat—if sometimes swampy— space as you could possibly want for constructing multiple fields. The heat? The mosquitoes? The lack of nightlife? All part of the daily life of a ballplayer. This is the Cleveland Indians' facility in Daytona Beach, Florida, in the early 1950s.

NICE WORK IF YOU COULD GET IT

A motley crew—apparently New York Giants beat writers—poses for the cameras in 1919. (Check out the "baseball cap" on the guy standing to the far right.) That's Fred Lieb, who wrote about baseball for more than six decades, in the front row, second from the left. The real Giants are conspicuous by their absence.

WISDOM OF THE AGES

Max Carey (right), who stole 738 bases in a twenty-year career (and led the National League ten times between 1913 and 1925), imparts some spring-training tips on baserunning posture and movement to the 1952 Cleveland Indians. But Carey was swimming against the tide: The 1950s was an era characterized by thick-necked sluggers slamming home runs, and in 1952 the Indians blasted 148 round-trippers but stole just forty-six bases as a team.

LEFT TURN

Frank Frisch adds the headfirst slide to his repertoire. In his prime, Frisch got to use all his varied sliding techniques. In 1923—probably his best season—he stroked 223 hits (including thirty-two doubles and ten triples), stole twenty-nine bases, and scored 116 runs. "If I needed one player to do the job of winning the game I most wanted to win," said Hall of Fame manager Joe McCarthy, "that player would be Frisch."

"THE MAN" AND THE BOYS

Stan Musial and three young residents of St. Petersburg, Florida, help celebrate "Let's All Play Ball Week," a nationwide program to encourage youth baseball through the American Legion, and Babe Ruth and Little Leagues. In the 1950s, before basketball, soccer, football, and other sports began nibbling away at youth baseball, the U.S. boasted more than ten thousand organized baseball leagues across the country.

WATCH THOSE FINGERS

Unenthusiastic New York Giants ballplayers practice their bunting skills. "There is no reason why a Major League batter should not be able to bunt," groused Hall of Famer George Sisler, who bunted up to fifty times a year and once hit .420. "But too many of them fail. This is largely because they dislike to bunt and won't take the trouble to learn."

BACK TO THE DRAWING BOARD

Sacrificial lamb Dick West shows how not to slide, in front of Cincinnati Reds manager Bill McKechnie (in glasses) and a handful of unimpressed players in this 1939 shot. The Reds must have learned something: They went 97–57 during the 1939 season to capture the N.L. pennant, before being swept away by Joe DiMaggio's dynastic Yankees in the World Series.

FROM HUMBLE BEGINNINGS...

...great double-play combinations grow: New York Giants star second baseman Frank Frisch (left) and sophomore shortstop Travis Jackson practice their exchange in a 1924 spring training session in Sarasota. Just three years earlier, Jackson (a native of Waldo, Arkansas) had been playing for Little Rock in the Southern League. "It held 4,500 people and I never saw a park that big," he recalled. "And there I was holding up my pants with a cotton rope."

NATURE'S BOUNTY

Jubilant Washington Senators enjoy a shipment of fresh produce at their training camp in Tampa, Florida, in 1925. The players had every right to be cheerful: They were coming off a 1924 season in which they edged the Yankees to win the A.L. pennant and then went on to defeat the New York Giants in one of the most thrilling World Series of all time—the one that gave the magnificent Walter Johnson his only championship.

THE GLUE

The heart of the great Brooklyn Dodgers teams of the early 1940s: infielders Arky Vaughan (third base), Dolph Camilli (first base), Billy Herman (second base), and Pee Wee Reese (shortstop) in Havana, Cuba, before the 1942 season. Along with outfielder Ducky Medwick, closer Hugh Casey, and others, the quartet led the Bums to a 104–50 record in 1942, but they finished second behind the St. Louis Cardinals, who boasted an astounding 106–48 mark.

MAN OF IRON

Lou Gehrig's follow-through reveals the impressive foundation of his power: his immensely strong arms and massive thighs and calves. Remarkably, given his fame now, Gehrig was underappreciated during his spectacular career with the Yankees, laboring for many years in Babe Ruth's shadow. "I'm not a headline guy," he said. "I know that as long as I was following Ruth to the plate I could have gone up there and stood on my head and nobody would have noticed the difference."

THE MECHANICAL MAN

Has there ever been a greater unsung player than the Detroit Tigers'
Charlie Gehringer? All he did during a nineteen-year career (1924–42)
was hit .320 overall, get more than two hundred hits seven times, slam
as many as sixty doubles, run out as many as nineteen triples, and play
near-flawless second base. Yet he displayed a seeming lack of emotion,
rarely changing expression on the field. But if he wasn't loved, he was
deeply respected. After he won the Most Valuable Player Award in
1937, the *Spalding Guide* said, "No player is more modest and more
deserving of such a compliment."

SURROUNDED BY SCRIBES

A disgruntled-looking John McGraw (front row, center) with a motley crew of friends and associates, including some of the many reporters who covered his New York Giants in the 1920s and 1930s. The group includes old-timer Bozeman Bulger of the *New York Evening World* (front row, second from left) and young up-and-comer Ken Smith of the *Mirror* (top right), who later became the director of the National Baseball Hall of Fame.

FORTY YEARS OF EXPERIENCE

New York Giants coach Hughie Jennings (left) and manager John McGraw give pointers to a young player identified only as "McGuire" at the Giants' spring training camp in San Antonio. Whatever he did, the feisty McGraw seemed to compel attention from photographers, writers, and fans alike. "Restless, aggressive, and quick-tempered, he would fight anybody—and frequently did," said writer Frank Graham. "The main idea," McGraw himself said, "is to win."

SAFE OR OUT?

Brilliant if conniving New York Highlanders first baseman Hal Chase tags teammate Irish McIlveen in an intramural benefit game played in Gray, Georgia, in spring 1909. The "A" team, including Chase, thirty-seven-year-old Willie Keeler, and other stars, whipped the "B" team, 10–2, but reporters on the scene were most excited by the play of a journeyman named Birdie Cree, who had three hits. Still, as the *New York Times* pointed out, "The game was not altogether serious, but the players had an enjoyable day. Chase played the last inning with a sweater in his right hand, and easily caught all the throws with the other hand."

ABOUT TO PULL THE TRIGGER

Fielding and running during spring training are all very well, but for a baseball player nothing's more fun than hitting. Babe Ruth, here preparing to blast one in a March 1925 contest, wielded the heaviest bat in the majors—occasionally an astonishing fifty-two ounces. "My theory is the bigger the bat, the faster the ball will travel," he said. And who would argue?

HEROES SHOULD NEVER GROW OLD

That's coach Christy Mathewson on the left, watching the high-spirited Giants play what looks like medicine-ball football during spring training in 1920. Matty was so handsome, so effortlessly charismatic, that it must have seemed he would never grow old. But a trip to France with the Chemical Corps during World War I had exposed him to poison gas, which injured his lungs, and by the time he returned—and was hired as a coach by the Giants—the years seemed to have caught up with him. Christy Mathewson died of tuberculosis in 1925, at the age of forty-five, just five years after this photo was taken.

Matty

Little Sport,
But not for the
Pitchers. San Antonio
1920

LIKE A GREEK GOD

Some players are so much fun to watch in batting practice that even their teammates stop what they're doing to take a look. As this photo shows, Lou Gehrig was one such player. What a feeling it must have been to have this man on your team, coming to the plate four or five times a game! "Gehrig's hands are like an iron vise and his arms are as big as many a man's leg," said the writer F. C. Lane, and he wasn't exaggerating.

BIRDS AND EGGS

Manager Red Schoendienst (left) serves 'em over easy to the St. Louis Cardinals' Dick Groat, coach Stan Musial, Bob Gibson, and Bill White during 1965 spring training in St. Petersburg. The stunt was undertaken in support of the U.S. Department of Agriculture, who pulled it together to call attention to the nation's oversupply of eggs. The Cardinals, still celebrating their World Series championship over the Yankees the year before, were game for the big cookout.

HOME COOKING

The New York Giants chow down on sandwiches and milk at their training camp in Augusta, Georgia, in 1928. Among those enjoying the meal are Carl Hubbell (left front) and a uniformless Travis Jackson (in front of the smiling woman). To ballplayers, the drudgery of spring training was often eased by the local families who came out to root for them—and who often took care of these young men, little older than children, who were so far from home.

SAY "CHEESE"!

Spring training might have been essential, but it also left a lot of free time—hours and hours spent with little to do while stuck somewhere in the then-undeveloped swamplands of Florida. Here Lou Gehrig entertains himself by "shooting" Yankees coach Art Fletcher. Take a look at Fletcher's pugnacious profile and you'll see why writer Frank Graham described him as a "firebrand, almost constantly embroiled with umpires and enemy players, and frequently fined and suspended in his National League days."

GRADUATION DAY

Some graduated and some got left behind: In the 1930s, a man named Ray E. Doan started an "All-Star Baseball School" that traveled from town to town, enlisting famous ballplayers as instructors. (In 1940, Babe Ruth provided hitting tips.) This photo, taken in Hot Springs, Arkansas, in the mid-1930s, shows such illustrious instructors as the St. Louis Cardinals' Dizzy Dean (far left) and St. Louis Browns manager Rogers Hornsby (kneeling, far right), who ran the school that year. The man in the dunce cap remains unidentified.

THE DAWN OF A NEW AGE

This fascinating photograph, taken in the spring of 1959, apparently shows every African-American player invited to camp that year by the St. Louis Cardinals. The Cardinals had hesitated to integrate, but by 1959, they were determined to make amends. Most of these men (front row: Marshall Bridges, George Crowe, Sam Jones, Ellis Burton, Dick Ricketts [the one white player pictured]; back row: Frank Barnes, Julio Gotay, Bill Harrell, Joe Durham, Bob Gibson) had short major-league careers at best. (The one future star, Gibson, was only a rookie.) But from such small steps giant leaps are taken: The Cards would soon be not only a deeply integrated team, but one led by intense, uncompromising African-American ballplayers such as Gibson, Lou Brock, Curt Flood, and Bill White.

SHUTTERHUG

Miller Huggins, the New York Yankees' mighty mite of a manager (1918-29), led the Bombers to six pennants and three championships in that stretch. Dwarfed by Babe Ruth's bulk and Lou Gehrig's stature, Hug was, in Frank Graham's words, "a scrawny little man, touched by baseball genius." He had to be a genius to manage a team with rowdies like the Babe and Leo Durocher on it. Who else but Huggins could have kept his dignity—and the respect of his players—after being hung out of a speeding train by Ruth during one road trip?

NEAR THE END OF THE LINE

The St. Louis Cardinals' Dizzy Dean limbers up in the spring of 1938. The caption of this newspaper photo reads, "Upon that powerful wing above hangs no small portion of the Cards' pennant hopes." But in truth Dean was nearly done, his career destroyed by an injury suffered during the previous season's All-Star Game. The Cards traded him to the Chicago Cubs before the season; relying mainly on guile, he went 7–1, then made an unsuccessful start in the 1938 Series. Two years later, at the age of thirty, the Great Dean's career was all but over.

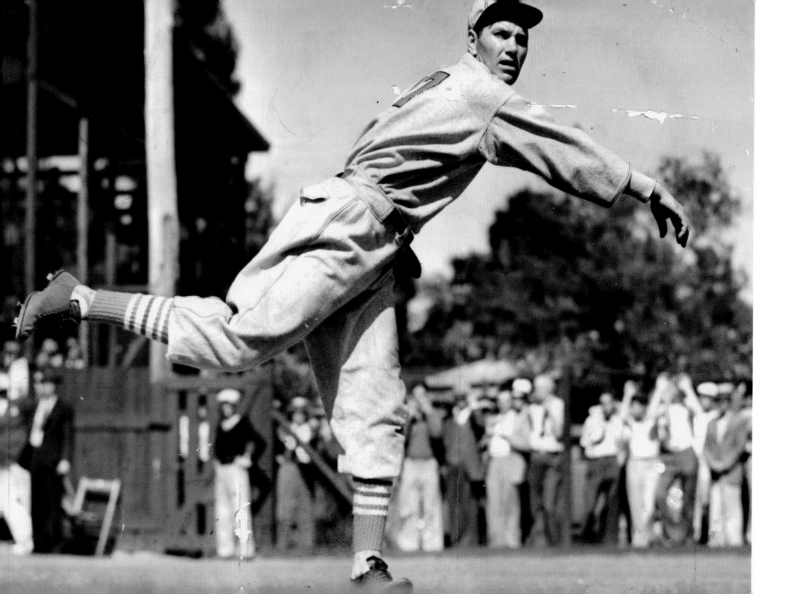

THE FACE OF A DYNASTY

Yankees great Whitey Ford talks things over with reporters after a spring-training game. It's hard to understate what a pitcher like Ford meant to the Yankees. He was unhurried, unflappable, cool under even the tensest conditions. Casey Stengel called him his "banty rooster," and the man he most wanted on the mound when it counted. And Mickey Mantle said, "Ford was the best clutch player I ever saw and one of the smartest."

LITTLE GENERAL

A remarkable number of great baseball managers have been fiery, pugnacious little guys, always willing to get into a scrap or take on even their own biggest stars. John McGraw was this type. So were Miller Huggins, Billy Martin, and Whitey Herzog. Add to the list Earl Weaver, pictured here early in his career as manager of the Baltimore Orioles. Going toe-to-toe with Jim Palmer, bellowing at an umpire, or even just sitting in the dugout, peering out at the goings-on in the field, Weaver led his great Orioles teams through a combination of brilliant strategy and unmatchable emotion. "I think there should be bad blood between all clubs," he once said.

"OUT!" "OUT!" "OUT!" "OUT!" "OUT!"

Aspiring arbiters receive invaluable instruction from Professor Bill McGowan (far right) at his renowned umpire school in Florida. The diminutive McGowan, a future Hall of Famer, left his mark on the American League for three decades before his death in 1954, at one point umpiring an astounding 2,541 consecutive games. But he didn't always do things by the book: While umpiring in the minor leagues as a young man, he once ejected a player from a game. The player refused to depart, saying, "You ain't big enough to throw me out." McGowan, 5' 9" at the most, said, "Well, sir, I have a surprise for you," and knocked the man cold with one punch.

BILL McGOWAN'S SCHOOL for UMPIRES
COCOA — 1949 — FLORIDA

GEARING UP

The Dodgers take on the Red Sox in an exhibition game just prior to the start of the 1943 season. That's Brooklyn player-manager Leo Durocher, his playing career dwindling at age thirty-seven, beating out a grounder as Sox first baseman Tony Lupien leaps for—and misses— the ball. "I loved being a playing manager," Durocher said later. "Christ, I was into everything; my wheels were spinning all the time."

THE ROAD HOME

Surrounded by elegantly attired fans, the equally well-dressed Chicago Cubs return from spring training in Tampa, Florida, in 1916. They're heading to their new ballpark, built on the frontiers of Chicago's North Side, far from the stockyards that characterized Chicago at the time. ("The North Side lacks the odors that have made the South Side so popular," commented Ring Lardner.) Originally named Weeghman Field and built to house the renegade Federal League's Chi-Feds, the park was eventually renamed Wrigley Field. It is the oldest National League ballpark still in use.

RIVALRY RENEWED

Six months after the Brooklyn Dodgers stunned the Yankees to win their first World Championship, the two teams met again in an exhibition game at Ebbets Field just prior to the start of the 1956 season. Here, Yankees rookie Jerry Lumpe beats out a throw from the Dodgers' Charlie Neal to Gil Hodges. Who would have guessed then that the Dodgers would be leaving town just two years hence?

CELEBRATING THIS SEASON AND LAST

Giants manager Bill Terry raises the American flag at the Polo Grounds in New York to commemorate the beginning of a new season and the Giants' 1937 National League pennant. Behind Terry stands Fiorello La Guardia, New York City's short, squat, and unashamedly colorful mayor. During his tenure (1934–45), La Guardia presided over an extraordinary era in New York City baseball history: Among them, the Giants, Dodgers, and Yankees won ten pennants and six World Series. The Series victories were all by the Yankees, of course.

HARBINGER OF THINGS TO COME

Charlie Root, Jr., perched in a baseball-shaped flower arrangement, greets his dad, Chicago Cubs pitcher and Opening Day starter Charlie, Sr., in Wrigley Field, April 16, 1929. (That's team owner William Wrigley on the far right.) The flowers were an expression of confidence that the Cubs, featuring such stars as Rogers Hornsby and Hack Wilson, would win the pennant. And they did, going 98–54 and cruising to the flag.

IN GOOD HANS

Honus (Hans) Wagner, center, and his Pittsburgh Pirates teammates raise the flag on a new season at Forbes Field in this undated photo that looks to have been taken in about 1910. In those years, the Wagner-led Pirates raised a lot of flags, winning four pennants between 1901 and 1909, and claiming the World Championship in 1909. "In all ways Wagner represents the greatest development of the model ball player," wrote the editors of the *Reach Guide* in 1905. "May his shadow never grow less!"

DON'T LET HIM OUT OF YOUR SIGHT

St. Louis Cardinals owner Sam Breadon and assorted family members keep an eye on team star—and onetime manager—Rogers Hornsby. As this picture reveals, Hornsby was a hothead, wearing out his welcome wherever he went. Hornsby lived for baseball, to the exclusion of reading, going to movies (both of which ruined your eyes, he said), and most other hobbies. "People ask me what I do in winter when there's no baseball," he said. "I'll tell you what I do. I stare out the window and wait for spring."

END OF THE RUN

The Yankees line up on Opening Day at the Stadium, April 11, 1963. The wreath commemorates their thrilling 1962 World Series victory over the San Francisco Giants—the Bombers' sixteenth World Series championship in twenty-seven years, and their last until 1977. "Very few players are able to recognize the exact moment when their skills start slipping," Mickey Mantle wrote. "It's not the same with a team, but it's close." And by 1963, even though their pennant run had two seasons to go, the Yankees were indeed slipping.

ON THE BRINK

The Yankees cluster on the field of spanking new Yankee Stadium on Opening Day of the 1923 season, where Commissioner Kenesaw Mountain Landis (center, with cane) distributes emblems celebrating their 1922 American League pennant. Yankees owner Jacob Ruppert stands to Landis' right. The Yankees had lost the 1922 World Series to the New York Giants, but in 1923 they would finally climb the mountain and win their first of many, many championships.

FRESH CROP FOR THE NEW SEASON

The Philadelphia Athletics' Eddie Collins, Connie Mack, and Ty Cobb pay a visit to the Reach baseball factory in Philadelphia in 1927. Each year, the factory produced about three million baseballs, including the official ones used by the American League. A. J. Reach himself, the company founder, had been a ballplayer and the first owner of the Philadelphia Phillies. Upon Reach's death, fellow sporting-goods impresario Albert Spalding said that "his services to the local public, as magnate, as advocate of 'popular priced ball,' and as a representative of all that is clean, honest, and dignified in the game, have been of inestimable value."

MEET MR. MET

A pair of admirers cuddle up to the New York Mets' mascot just prior to Opening Day, 1965. For fans of that dreadful (yet adorable) team, favorites—whether it be Mr. Met, bonus babies Ed Kranepool and Ron Swoboda, or Manager Casey Stengel—were almost as important as the game on the field. Good thing: These two women and millions of others had watched the team go 53–109 in 1964, and would see them disimprove to 50–112 (forty-seven games out of first place!) in 1965.

CLOSE TO THE ACTION

Fans crowd the field for an Opening Day game between the American League's Boston Pilgrims and the New York Highlanders at Boston's Huntington Avenue Grounds in the early 1900s. The A.L. was founded by Ban Johnson in 1901 with a specific goal of providing a cleanly played game for fans accustomed to the rowdy, vulgar, often drunken crowds (and players) of the National League. And Johnson succeeded: Both leagues soon featured a more family-friendly product.

…E …ND …AM…, AMER. LEAGUE PARK, BET. BOSTON & N.Y.

THE YOUTH OF AMERICA

How could fans have gone so nuts over a team that was lucky to win a third of its games? Forty years later, New York's love affair with the early Mets remains hard to explain, except as a reaction to the dynastic Yankees, a desire for a National League team in New York after a four-year absence, and the presence of so many fresh-faced kids and under-talented veterans gamely battling better teams. Here, Casey Stengel (in his final season as manager) lectures Ed Kranepool (fourth from left) and the rest of his starting lineup on Opening Day, 1965.

SEASONED VETS

Casey Stengel (far right) in happy times, with the ever-powerful, veteran-heavy Yankees of 1959. But Casey's tenure with the Bombers was coming to an end. After leading the team to just a 79–75 record that year (their worst mark since 1925!), he got them back to the Series in 1960. But this was the Series won by Bill Mazeroski's epochal home run, and after the last game the aging Stengel was let go by the Yankees. "I'll never make the mistake of being seventy again," he famously said.

FIRST IN WAR...

You gotta pay your dues. After he starred for the "Wait Till Next Year" Brooklyn Dodgers, and before he achieved baseball immortality as manager of the 1969 Miracle Mets, Gil Hodges (#14) helmed the woeful Washington Senators ("First in war, first in peace, last in the American League"). But though he never won more than seventy-six games in a season with the Senators, the team improved every season from 1963 through 1967 under his quiet but strong-willed guidance. In the words of writer Arnold Hano, Hodges was "a patient, devoted man with a fine heart" who didn't have very many good teams to work with, but he was a great manager.

THE PROFESSOR AND THE PRESIDENT

All smiles, President Dwight Eisenhower shakes hands with Yankees manager Casey Stengel at Washington's Griffith Stadium, Opening Day, 1953. (That's V.P. Richard Nixon looking over Eisenhower's shoulder, and Senator Lyndon Johnson in the white hat, on the left.) Later that year, after the Yankees had captured their fifth consecutive American League pennant, Ike let his true feelings show. "On the day of the opening game [of the World Series]," Mickey Mantle recalled, "President Eisenhower and former President Truman both told reporters they hoped we would lose. That may have been the only issue they agreed on."

THE CZAR IS WATCHING

Judge Kenesaw Mountain Landis, the first baseball commissioner, tosses out the first ball at an unidentified game from the 1920s. Taking over after the 1919 Black Sox scandal almost ruined the game, Landis was chartered by the owners to earn back the fans' trust in baseball's integrity—and that's exactly what he did. To the public, Judge Landis was the most severe and upright of men, but according to writer Fred Lieb, the private Landis could be quite different. "After hours, when the Judge could feel free to let his shaggy hair down, he liked to imitate the speech, grammar, and mannerisms of the club owners who employed him," Lieb recalled.

PLAY BALL!

New York Mets pitcher Jack Fisher throws the first pitch ever tossed in Shea Stadium, on April 17, 1964. The Pittsburgh Pirates' Dick Schofield waits for the ball to arrive. After two years in the cacophonous old Polo Grounds, the Mets were proud of their shiny new stadium, but not all were won over. "No longer snug in a shoebox, my companions and I were ants perched on the sloping lip of a vast, shiny soup plate, and we were lonelier than we liked," wrote Roger Angell of Shea in *The Summer Game.*

TY COBB'S DREAM

Everything would be easy if all bases were unguarded. In real life, of course, something—a glove, a foot, a shin, the ball—almost always served as an obstacle between Ty Cobb and the bag. That's when fans and opposing players saw the real Georgia Peach, the ferocious competitor who would come roaring into a base with spikes flying. "All you've got to do is give me room to get in there and it'll be all right," he told pitcher Smokey Joe Wood. "But if you don't give me room, I'll cut my way in."

FORGOTTEN DYNASTY

No, they didn't have a Ruth and Gehrig, but the St. Louis Cardinals' lineup in the 1940s was nothing to shake a bat at. Johnny Mize (far left) was "the TNT guy of the group," as one newspaper put it, and he was joined by (left to right) Enos Slaughter, Jimmy Brown, Walker Cooper, and Terry Moore. In 1941, when this photograph was taken, the Cards posted ninety-seven wins but finished second. In 1942–44, however, the team won 106, 105, and 105 games, capturing three straight N.L. pennants and two World Series championships. Yet these Cardinals teams are little remembered today, perhaps because their greatest glories took place during World War II, when many of the game's biggest stars were in the service.

THE MOODY SPLINTER

Ted Williams heads for first and another base hit, and the forlorn catcher dreams of the ball reaching his glove. "The Splendid Splinter" was unrelenting in his pursuit of hitting perfection, often alienating himself from fans, writers, and even teammates in the process. "If he has a good stretch, he can be amiable, a good conversationalist, with an intelligent grasp of his own problems, those of his team, his country, the world," said Fred Lieb. "But when things go into reverse, Williams suffers moods when he frequently goes into a blue funk."

THE INTIMIDATOR

Batters should have earned medals for bravery simply for hanging in at home plate against Bob Gibson. No pitcher in baseball history felt more ownership over the 60'6" between the mound and the plate. "It is not something I earned or acquired or bought," he wrote of his brilliance in his autobiography, *From Ghetto to Glory*. "It is a gift. It was something that was given to me—just like the color of my skin."

CONNIE AND THE GIRLS

Connie Mack (center) poses with the Kenosha Comets of the All-American Girls Professional Baseball League, later immortalized in the movie *A League of Their Own*. The editors of *Baseball Magazine* were among the enthusiastic fans of the AAGPBL. "The players themselves are wholesome girls as feminine as your mother. They play a good game of ball and a clean one," raved an editorial in March 1947. "They are continually drawing flighty bobbysoxers away from dingy dance halls of questionable repute to seats in the ball parks. And when these youngsters come home and rave about their new heroes, female stars of the diamond instead of zootsuiters, mother is naturally impressed and relieved."

DID HE OR DIDN'T HE?

In a play that was famous in its time, Ty Cobb was vilified for spiking the Philadelphia Athletics' beloved Frank "Home Run" Baker on the arm in a 1909 game. Scrawled on the back of the print of this photograph is the fiery Cobb's rejoinder. "I have resented this charge since 1909," he wrote in a spiky, impatient hand. "[Baker] is clearly on the offensive, blocking me away from third base. I am on inside trying to get to the bag. My foot has passed by his arm and yet his arm was not knocked aside. I am trying only to reach the bag with my toe. He had a slight cut on the forearm, never lost an innings play."

DIZZY AND THE BIRDS

Dizzy Dean (in suit) flocks with a new generation of St. Louis Cardinals stars (left to right): Stan Musial, Enos Slaughter, and Terry Moore. All but Moore are now in the Hall of Fame, but by all accounts Moore was the glue that helped hold together the superb Cardinals teams of the 1930s and 1940s. One of the greatest center fielders of all time, he was also a quiet leader of a team with more than its share of free spirits, malcontents, and assorted other misfits.

ON THE OUTSIDE LOOKING IN

The Cubs' Ron Santo hangs in there at third base as Rusty Staub barrels toward him. Santo was a strong fielder (he won five Gold Gloves) and hitter (342 career home runs in an era when pitchers dominated), yet the memory of his accomplishments has faded since his playing days ended in 1974. Perhaps if the Cubs had held off the Miracle Mets in 1969 and had then gone on to win the World Series, Santo's grace and skill would be more vividly remembered today.

SUPERSTARS

That's Ted Williams on the left, Hank Greenberg on the right, and skinny young John F. Kennedy in the suit in this remarkable 1946 picture. (The player facing the camera is Eddie Pellagrini, who donated the photo.) JFK never lost his affection for baseball, perhaps due in part to this meeting with two baseball gods. Later, when as president he was told that more people went to symphonies than baseball games, he remarked, "This may be viewed as an alarming statistic, but I think that both baseball and the country will endure."

AN AGELESS STAR

Still in remarkable shape at forty, Ted Williams (left) lends support to young slugger Jackie Jensen during a 1958 season in which Williams hit .328 with twenty-six home runs. Pictures like this were rarely published during Williams' career, when the press harped on his sometimes grim intensity, his refusal to tip his cap after a home run, and his overall joylessness in public. "It is unfortunate for Ted that his kindly acts, his thoughtful deeds never receive the publicity accorded his sulks," lamented writer Tom Meany at the time.

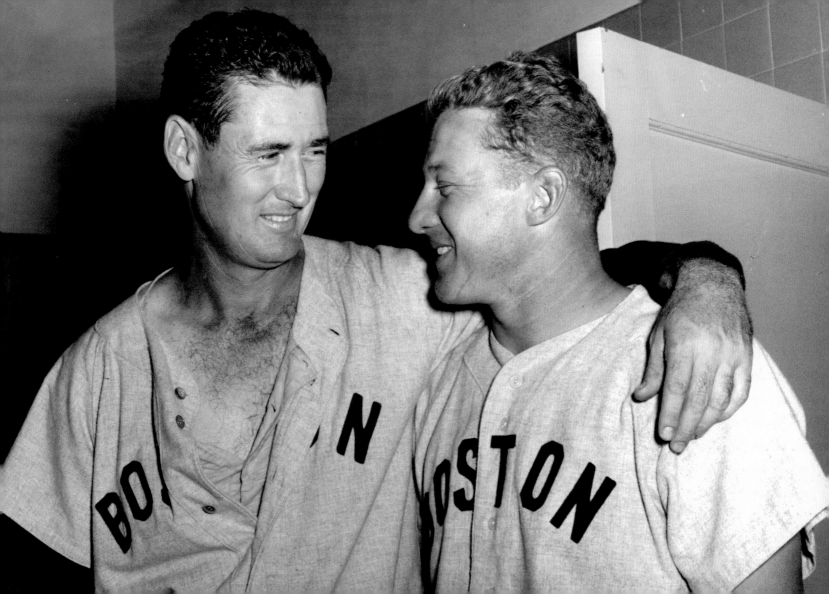

TRIPLE-CROWN TALENT

Playing the heart of his career during an era when pitchers ruled the game, Frank Robinson of the Cincinnati Reds and, later, the Baltimore Orioles and three other teams, still managed to slam 586 career home runs, win the Triple Crown in 1966, and carry both the Reds (in 1961) and the O's (in 1966, 1969, 1970, and 1971) to the World Series. He was that good, and he knew it. "I don't see anyone in the major leagues today who combines both the talent and the intensity that I had," he said after being elected to the Hall of Fame in 1982.

A MOMENT TO REMEMBER FOREVER

A young fan gets to meet his idol, Joe DiMaggio (left), as Yankees manager Joe McCarthy (right) and Postmaster General James Farley look on. Such brief meetings must have reminded DiMaggio of the baseball-mad childhood he shared with Dominic and Vince, his future major-leaguer brothers. "If anyone wants to know why three kids in one family made it to the big leagues they just had to know how we helped each other and how much we practiced back then," he told writer Bill Gutman. "We did it every minute we could."

CALM BEFORE THE STORM

Feisty managers Miller Huggins of the St. Louis Cardinals (left) and John McGraw of the New York Giants meet with umpire William Brennan before a 1913 game at the Polo Grounds. The seasons their two teams were having couldn't have been more dramatically different: The Cards were on their way to a 51–99 record and a last-place finish, while the Giants were headed to a 101–51 mark and the National League pennant. Less than a decade later, the two men would be facing each other in a trio of World Series, as McGraw's Giants took on Huggins' New York Yankees in 1921, 1922, and 1923.

THREE SLUGGERS

Roger Maris (left) looks milder and more modest than either Willie Mays or Mickey Mantle in this photograph. Perhaps his appearance explains why Maris never got the respect or affection he deserved for surpassing Babe Ruth's home-run record in 1961. With their knotted forearms and strong jawlines, Mays and Mantle looked the part of the mighty hero, but the diffident Maris simply didn't have the same panache. "It didn't take long for Maris to be stamped as not being a New York kind of guy," Mantle said of Maris' arrival with the Yankees. "He was a Fargo, North Dakota, kind of guy."

EL PRODUCTO

Willie Mays uncorks a powerful throw from the outfield. In the field, on the bases, or at bat, Mays carved out a reputation as perhaps the greatest all-around player of all time. He was also the most fun to watch, playing the game with a joyful abandon that was impossible to resist, even if you were a fan of the other team. "Everything about him delighted me," said his longtime manager, Leo Durocher, and countless others felt the same way.

WILLIE LAUNCHES ANOTHER ONE

Willie Mays, the catcher, the umpire, the fans, and some disconsolate (but unsurprised) Mets stuck in the dugout watch as Mays follows through on another crushing swing. He always attributed his extraordinary upper-body muscles to his stint in the Army in the early 1950s. "I loved the calisthenics," he said. "I think all those push-ups I did made my arms bigger."

JUST THROW THE BALL

All taut tendons and forward thrust, Tom Seaver uncorks a pitch. Perhaps the greatest pitcher of his generation—he won 311 games and three Cy Young Awards in a twenty-year career—the demanding and self-confident Seaver was the single biggest reason why the Mets went from being a lovable joke in 1962 to a World Series champion just seven years later. "Arriving two years ago to join a hopeless collection of habitual cellar mice," Roger Angell wrote of Seaver in 1969, "he made it clear at once that losing was unacceptable."

POWER

He missed crushing this one (see the dirt fly as the ball bounces in front of the plate), but Harmon Killebrew didn't miss many during his prime years with the Washington Senators and Minnesota Twins. Massive, brooding, the quintessential power hitter, "Killer" slammed 573 home runs and drove in 1,584 in the course of a twenty-two-year career. He led the league in homers six times, and though he never hit as many as fifty round-trippers in a season, he exceeded forty an astonishing eight times. Though not the most colorful or quotable of players, and despite playing most of his career with a competitive team that was never quite good enough to capture a championship, Killebrew was elected to the Hall of Fame in 1984.

PERFECT STYLE

Luis Aparicio employs a perfect slide to score a run. Arriving on the major-league scene in 1956—an era when few players stole bases—Aparicio helped revitalize a game that had grown over-dependent on big bruisers slugging home runs. He led the league with twenty-one stolen bases in his first year, and continued to lead it for eight more seasons in a row. By the time he retired in 1973, Aparicio had witnessed the full flowering of the baserunning revolution, with the arrival of such speedsters as Maury Wills, Lou Brock, and Bert Campaneris.

THE CATCHER'S LOT

Is there a more thankless job in baseball than catcher? With the exception of the occasional superstar (Yogi Berra, Johnny Bench, Carlton Fisk), most backstops labor in obscurity punctuated by sore knees, collisions, and the occasional passed ball. (Even in the World Series, catchers are better known for their failures, like Mickey Owen's dropped third strike and Ernie Lombardi's "snooze," than for any heroics.) The designated victim in this photo is the Pittsburgh Pirates' Tom Padden, here seeking to be an immovable object against the St. Louis Cardinals' Terry Moore's unstoppable force.

ON THE BRINK

The National League's Boston Beaneaters pose in 1900, a year before an aggressive businessman named Ban Johnson decided to take on the august but struggling N.L. by forming a new major league. Perhaps his most in-your-face move was to establish a team in Boston, long dominated by the Beaneaters. ("In a baseball sense," wrote Fred Lieb, "that was 'the shot heard round the world.'") The American League began play in 1901, and almost immediately the Boston entry (usually called the Americans) became one of the league's strongest teams. In 1903, they captured the pennant and went on to defeat the heavily favored Pittsburgh Pirates in the first true World Series, proving once and for all that the American League could keep up with its "big brother."

ODD MAN OUT

This is a rare photo of three of the most famous names in baseball history, a trio of Chicago Cubs Hall of Famers forever wedded in fans' memories. Starting second from the left are Joe Tinker, Johnny Evers, and Frank Chance. While Tinker-to-Evers-to-Chance was the famed Cubs double-play combination, of course the three didn't form Chicago's entire infield. On the far left is the fourth infielder, third baseman Harry Steinfeldt, who was cursed with a name that didn't scan. He was a good ballplayer, though, hitting .327 and leading the league in hits and RBI in 1906, and playing an important role in the Cubs' three consecutive World Series appearances in 1906–08.

PEERLESS LEADER

Some men just look like ballplayers, such as Frank Chance, Chicago Cubs player-manager during the first decade of the twentieth century. He began his playing career as a catcher before moving to first base, a move he greeted with great reluctance. "He didn't want to play first base and he did not believe he could play the position," recalled sports-writer Hugh Fullerton. "He even threatened to quit baseball rather than make the change." But reason—and an increase in salary—prevailed, and Chance went on to guide his team to two World Championships.

DOWNTIME

Members of the Philadelphia Athletics and New York Highlanders get through the pregame hours together before an April 1908 match pitting the two dreadful teams. While the Detroit Tigers, Cleveland Naps, Chicago White Sox, and St. Louis Browns fought through one of the greatest pennant races in baseball history—the Tigers eventually captured the flag by a mere half-game over the Indians—the Athletics and Highlanders combined to go 119–188. The Athletics' time was almost at hand, though: The team would vault to second place in 1909 and all the way to first, and World Series victories, in 1910 and 1911.

THE EYES OF AN ARBITER

He looked like he came out of the womb ready to call you out on strikes. These are two photos of the great umpire Bill Klem, a towering figure in early-twentieth-century baseball. Klem's response when reporters showed him a photograph proving he'd blown a call? "Gentlemen, he was out," intoned Bill, "because I said he was out." But there was one way to get Klem's goat: Call him "Catfish." *That* would get you thrown out of the game pronto.

PORTRAIT OF A STAR

The Cleveland Indians' Napoleon Lajoie poses with his war club, on his way to a lifetime .338 batting average, 3,242 hits, and a plaque in the Hall of Fame. When asked his secrets of hitting, he said, "The pitcher's thoughts are his own.... I don't know what he is thinking about and I don't care. It doesn't matter to me whether he throws a curve or a fast one so long as he gets the ball over the plate where I can reach it."

PLENTY SMART

Pitcher Luther Taylor of the New York Giants was known during his 1900–1908 career as "Dummy," due to the fact that he was deaf and mute. But he still managed to get his point across whenever he disagreed with an umpire's call. Having taught his Giants teammates sign language, Taylor was able to express himself without the unfortunate ump understanding a word. But Taylor never reckoned on Hank O'Day, a hot-tempered umpire of the time. Without telling anyone, O'Day went home one off-season and spent months learning sign language. The first time Taylor and the Giants started talking with their hands, O'Day fired back with some choice sign language of his own, threw Taylor out of the game, and fined the startled pitcher $50.

THE SENATORPEDE

No one ever took credit for having the silly idea of lining up the Washington Senators this way (in size order!) for a 1909 team picture. Nor is it clear why young Walter Johnson (far right) is wearing a suit. Perhaps it's so his bowler hat will make him the "tallest" man on the team. "He had a slovenly walk, he was slew-footed and his arms dangled at his side like two cuts of flabby fire hose," wrote Joe Williams of Johnson. "But when he swung into action he was a blur of physical poetry."

WASHINGTON BASE BALL CLUB.
1909.

COOL AS ICE

Frank Graham wrote that Christy Mathewson (third from right) was "a Greek god in flannels and he had the effortless motion and the speed, curve ball and control that baseball scouts dream of in a pitcher." Matty and his Giants teammates look ready for action in this undated photograph. Mathewson, quiet and always well-mannered, inspired awe among all who saw him pitch.

THE DETROIT BASEBALL SOCIETY

Ty Cobb (second row, second from right), manager Hughie Jennings (second row, fourth from right), and the rest of the Detroit Tigers attempt to prove that baseball is a gentleman's game. For Cobb, dressing up like this must have been torture. As Bill James said of Cobb's expression in many off-the-field photographs: "You can see it in his face, I think, that if he could just put on a uniform and go out on the field it would be such a relief to him, out where manners and taste and style were all defined by bases gained and bases lost."

OUT OF SIGHT

Their uniforms were shabby and their gloves battered, but man, could they play. Smokey Joe Williams (far right), John Henry Lloyd (fourth from right), Spottswood Poles (third from left), and other Negro leagues superstars got by in the Cuban Winter League in 1913. Our image of these brilliant players will always be dim because they played before the breaking of the color barrier. "[S]uppose Willie Mays had never had a chance to play big league. Then I were to come to you and try to tell you about Willie Mays," Monte Irvin told writer Anthony Connor in *Baseball for the Love Of It*. "Now this is the way it is with Cool Papa Bell. This is the way it is with Buck Leonard…. I'm thinking about Smokey Joe Williams and Mule Suttles and Biz Mackay, and right on down the line."

THE GREAT JOSH

Josh Gibson, star catcher of the Negro National League Homestead Grays, rounds third in a game at Washington's Griffith Stadium. "There is a catcher that any big league club would love. His name is Gibson... he can do anything," said the great Walter Johnson. "He hits the ball a mile. And he catches so easy he might as well be in a rocking chair. Throws like a rifle. Too bad this Gibson is a colored fellow." Gibson, a short man with extraordinarily powerful arms and broad shoulders, was by all accounts one of the greatest hitters of all time, and would likely have hit more home runs than any other catcher in baseball history—if he'd only gotten the chance.

PORTRAIT OF A PLAYING MANAGER

Shortstop Joe Cronin, future manager of the Boston Red Sox, whom he led to four second-place finishes and one A.L. pennant between 1938 and 1946. The deal that brought Cronin to the Sox from the Washington Senators in return for $250,000 was baseball's most talked-about sale since Boston gave Babe Ruth to the Yankees for $24 worth of trinkets, or a handful of magic beans, or whatever it was. What made Cronin's move particularly piquant was that he was married to the daughter of the Senators' owner, Clark Griffith, the man responsible for the sale! "Maybe old Griffith has something," commented one newspaper columnist at the time. "I wish I could sell my son-in-law for $250,000."

ROBINS TRIUMPHANT

They're little remembered today, but these four infielders—first baseman Jake Daubert, second baseman George Cutshaw, shortstop Ivy
Olson, and third baseman Harry Mowrey—helped lead the Brooklyn
Robins (later the Dodgers) to the National League pennant in 1916, the
year this photograph was taken. Unfortunately, the Robins' World
Series opponents were the Boston Red Sox—led by a magnificent
young pitcher named Babe Ruth—and the Series proved to be no contest, with the Sox winning in five games.

OL' PETE

Grover Cleveland "Pete" Alexander warms up for the start of another game in another season during a turbulent career that lasted two decades. Today, all most people remember about Alexander is that he drank too much, that he struck out the Yankees' Tony Lazzeri with the bases loaded to help the St. Louis Cardinals win the 1926 World Series, or that Ronald Reagan played him in a movie. What they don't often remember is how good Pete was, and for how long. He won twenty-eight games as a rookie in 1911, won more than thirty games three times in his career, and went 21–10 in 1927, when he was forty years old. His 373 career victories rank him third (tied with Christy Mathewson) all time, behind only Cy Young and Walter Johnson.

DUCK!!!

A rare victims'-eye view of the incomparable Babe Ruth. (One assumes the photographer fled to safety as soon as the exposure was taken.) This image gives a good sense of the mammoth "war club" that Ruth brought to the plate, and also how tightly he gripped it. "When I am out after a homer, I try to make mush out of this solid ash handle," Ruth said. "You know, in boxing, when you hit a man your fist generally stops right there, but it is possible to hit a man so hard that your fist doesn't stop. When I carry through with the bat, it is for the same reason."

COMFORT ZONE

What baseball manager didn't envy Miller Huggins (center) the good fortune of being able to trot Babe Ruth and Lou Gehrig out on the field together year after year? This undated photograph looks to have been taken circa 1927, when Ruth slugged his sixty home runs, Gehrig merely hit .373 with forty-seven home runs and 175 RBI, and the Yankees went 110–44 before slaughtering the overmatched Pittsburgh Pirates in a Series sweep. But Huggins' job wasn't as easy as it looked. "With a team chock full of prima donnas, Huggins has had the worst managerial task in the major leagues," wrote sportswriter Joseph Vila in 1923. "The players dislike him and the fans ignore him."

KNEEL BEFORE US

The Washington Senators' (and, later, Minnesota Twins') four big sluggers strode like colossi over the American League for a couple of years in the late 1950s. In 1959, for example, Jim Lemon, Bob Allison, Harmon Killebrew, and Roy Sievers combined for 126 home runs and 339 RBI—and not a one of them had his best season. But the Senators' hapless ownership didn't provide enough support for their power hitters, the team never quite made the transition from contenders to champions, and today only Hall of Famer Killebrew is widely remembered.

GRIP OF STEEL

Mel Ott shows off his powerful slugger's hands. Ott came to the New York Giants in 1926, when he was just seventeen years old, and manager John McGraw gave the boy wonder just sixty at bats that year, 163 the next. But he never let anyone else touch the prospect he called "the best looking young player at the bat in my time with the Club." When Casey Stengel, then managing in the minors, asked if he could use Ott for a season, McGraw gave an emphatic thumbs-down. "No minor-league manager is going to ruin him," he told Casey. "And that goes for you too." Smart move: In a twenty-two-year career, Ott hit 511 home runs and drove in 1,860 runs, helping carry the Giants to three pennants and one World Series championship.

FORGOTTEN SUPERSTAR

Quick—who held the record for the most hits in a single season before Ichiro Suzuki broke it in 2004? No, it's not Ty Cobb or Rogers Hornsby or Lou Gehrig or the Babe. It's the man shown sliding safely in this photograph: George Sisler, one of today's forgotten stars. Sisler was on his way to one of the greatest hitting careers of all time—in 1920-22 he *averaged* 240 hits a year—when he contracted a sinus or eye infection. He was never the same consistent hitter again, though he did end up with 2,812 hits and election to the Hall of Fame. Oh, and that record, which stood for more than eighty years? 257 hits in 1920.

THE BIG CAT

One of the many players whose career numbers were significantly diminished by more than three years of service in the military during World War II, Johnny Mize was one of the most feared sluggers in baseball. Before heading back to the Giants after the war, he knew he had to get in shape. "On an island in the Pacific, he went into a tin hut at high noon each day. With all openings closed, the inside of that hut was just about the hottest spot in that part of the world," wrote Ira L. Smith in *Baseball's Famous First Basemen*. "Mize had a mat on the floor and did a variety of strenuous exercises. He came out of that self-imposed conditioning program in fine physical condition to resume his baseball career."

ZACK ATTACK

A lifetime .317 hitter with 2,884 hits from 1909 to 1927, Zack Wheat reached a pinnacle in 1924, when he lashed 212 hits and hit for a .375 average. Playing much of his career in an era with inflated batting averages (.400 wasn't uncommon) and prodigious home-run totals (his career high was sixteen), Wheat usually avoided much notice. Asked to describe his great 1924 season, he had a succinct reply: "I developed a contempt for pitchers," he said. The Hall of Fame didn't have contempt for Wheat, making space on its wall for his plaque in 1959.

PORTRAIT OF A BYGONE AGE

Old baseball photographs—like this one of the New York Highlanders (soon to be the Yankees) circa 1911—provide an invaluable glimpse of a world as long gone as one of Babe Ruth's home runs. Note how tiny the glove is on the player on the left: No wonder teams regularly made more than 300 errors in a season, three times as many as modern teams do. The bats, laid out on the ground instead of neatly stacked in a rack, would never pass today's pine-tar tests. And the fans are not only overwhelmingly male but also overwhelmingly well dressed, two baseball traditions that are gone forever.

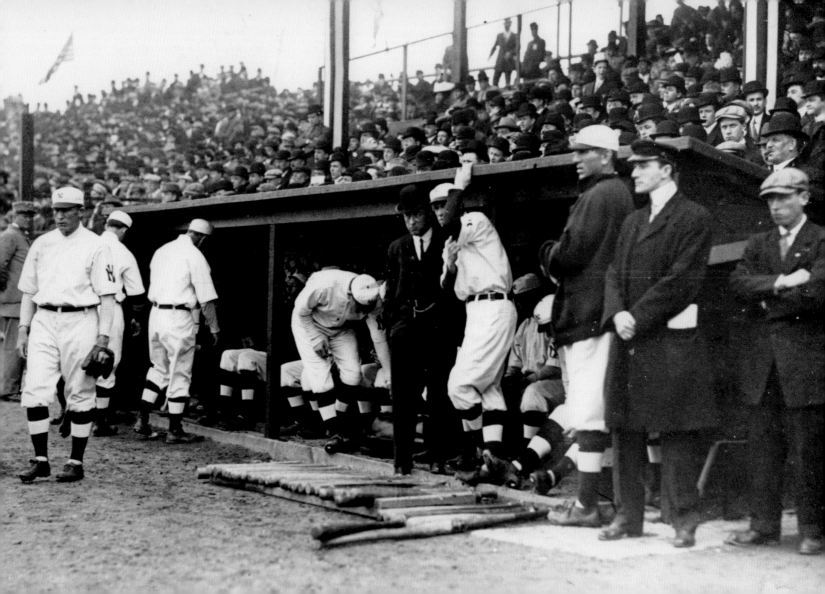

THE DOMINATOR

Pete Alexander pitched brilliantly for most of two decades, and his best years took place with the Philadelphia Phillies. Between 1911 and 1917, he went 190–88 with the Phillies, winning thirty or more games each year from 1915 to 1917. "It is doubtful if there was ever a smoother pitcher than Alexander," wrote Tom Meany. "He worked without exertion while warming up and when he went to the mound he pitched with the same easy motion.... There were no three-hour ballgames when Alexander was pitching."

CONFERENCE CALL

"Home plate is over there. I'll be standing behind it." Umpires instruct the Highlanders and Tigers—including Detroit manager Hughie Jennings (left), superstar Ty Cobb, and an unidentified New York player—in ground rules before a game at New York's Hilltop Park. In most photos of the time, Jennings seems to be smiling, but maybe he's gritting his teeth: It couldn't have been easy managing an underachieving team that starred the irascible Cobb.

THE SHIFT

After years of watching Ted Williams pull the ball through the infield into right, player-manager Lou Boudreau of the Cleveland Indians had had enough. In a 1946 game, he piled all four infielders to the right of second base. Ted walked that time but was hitless in the game, and other teams soon picked up the habit. They challenged Williams to change his swing and hit the ball the other way, but that wasn't the Splinter's style. "I *didn't* give in, *wouldn't* give in, *wouldn't* give up my power game," Williams, ever defiant, said later of what he called the "damn Williams Shift." Given that he led the league in batting four times after the shift came into use, opposing managers clearly should have gone back to the drawing board.

JIM SEEREY
CENTER FIELD

HANK EDWARDS
RIGHT FIELD

GEORGE CASE
LEFT FIELD

KEN KELTNER
THIRD BASEMAN

LOU BOUDREAU
SHORTSTOP

JACK CONWAY
SECOND BASE

JIMMY WASDELL
FIRST BASE

CHARLEY EMBREE
PITCHER

JOE CRONIN
MGR.

WILLIAMS
AT THE BAT

JORDAN
CATCHER

The Cleveland Indians placed themselves
in this unorthodox manner in an attempt
to keep Ted Williams from getting another hit.
-- and then they walked Williams on
four straight balls.

CLEVELAND vs. RED SOX
FENWAY PARK, JULY 14, 1946

Eddie Collins
from
Des Wachsmoth
August 1946

THE GEORGIA PEACH

"My idea of a real batter is a man who can choke up on the bat when he feels like it or slug from the handle when it is necessary," opined Ty Cobb. "A combination of proper handling of the bat and good footwork will go a long way to offset any system of pitching that has ever been devised." Cobb's then-famous split-handed grip helped him to his life-time .366 batting average and 4,189 hits. Only a few other players emulated this strange style; perhaps more should have.

STILL SWINGING

Taking a few hacks as manager of the Washington Senators after his playing career ended, Gil Hodges displays the form that enabled him to launch 370 home runs, mostly for the Dodgers. He was perhaps the single most beloved player of his generation, the darling of fans through thick and thin. "Only a few players are comfortable accepting the public's adoration, and trying to meet the standard of conduct that goes along, the expectations of being The Nation's Son," Bill James writes. Hodges, as player and manager alike, was one of the few to fit the bill.

SHOOTING STAR

Al Rosen couldn't break into the Cleveland Indians' lineup until he was twenty-six years old, and injuries short-circuited his career when he was barely past thirty. But for five seasons, he was one of the most feared sluggers in the majors, hitting as high as .336, exceeding 100 RBI five times (with a high of 145, the most of any player in the 1950s), and slugging as many as forty-three home runs. Given a normal full-length career, he might have gone down in history as the greatest third baseman of all, as good as, or better than, Mike Schmidt or George Brett.

SUPERSTAR AND JOURNEYMEN

On the left is Hall of Famer Frank Frisch, who spent a decade with the St. Louis Cardinals and led them to four pennants. Next to him are Earl Smith and George Harper, two useful if unspectacular role players with seven previous teams between them. In a stroke of mutual luck, both Smith and Harper stopped by St. Louis just long enough to play in the 1928 World Series—where they and the other Cardinals were swept away by the magnificent Ruth-Gehrig Yankees. (Luck will take you only so far.)

THREE FOR THE HALL

In 1928 three of the greatest players ever to play the game ended up on the Philadelphia Athletics. Ty Cobb (left), Tris Speaker (center), and Eddie Collins had an astounding sixty-six years of major-league play behind them, but all the experience in the world is nothing to the ravages of time. The 1928 season would be the last for Speaker (who hit .267, nearly eighty points below his career batting average) and Cobb (who managed to hit .323 in 353 at bats), while Collins, who hung around for a couple more years, batted only thirty-three times. The trio just missed a last hurrah in the World Series, as the Athletics fell short of the Yankees for the 1928 pennant.

HEADING HOME

George Sisler sees the promised land—home plate—waiting before him. Though little remembered now, Sisler (he of the .420 batting average in 1922) was considered an all-time great during and soon after his career. When the Baseball Hall of Fame opened its doors in 1939, there to mark the occasion were such immortals as Babe Ruth, Ty Cobb, Tris Speaker, Walter Johnson, Cy Young—and George Sisler, one of the first players ever to be enshrined. By the way, the glove wasn't there by accident. Until a 1954 rule change, players routinely left their gloves on the field when they headed for the dugout.

FULL OF BEANS

That's ever-confident George Earnshaw on the right, facing down the cameraman, alongside Baltimore Oriole teammate Clayton Sheedy. The minor-league Orioles, led by Lefty Grove and other future major-league stars, were clearly the equal of many major-league teams in the early 1920s. But Earnshaw, shown here in 1924—when the Orioles went 117–48—clearly knew he was headed to an even bigger stage. Joining Connie Mack's Philadelphia Athletics in 1928, he was a superb, aggressive pitcher from 1929 to 1931 (winning a total of sixty-seven games) and a prime reason why the Athletics won three straight pennants and two World Series during those years.

IN THE LUMBERYARD

The Chicago Cubs' Hack Wilson (left) and Rogers Hornsby examine the tools of their trade. In 1929 each smashed thirty-nine home runs, and the Cubs rolled to the National League pennant, only to be flattened by the Philadelphia Athletics in the World Series. Within two years, however, the most productive period of both of these stars' careers would be over.

THEY CAME AFTER

Just a few years after the great Chicago White Sox team of the late 1910s was torn apart by the Black Sox scandal, the team was largely composed of semi-anonymous, more or less talented players like these: Bibb Falk, Earl Sheely, and Willie Kamm. The Sox weren't exactly *bad* (in 1926, when this photo was taken, they went 81–72 and finished fifth), but it would be 1959—a full forty years after the scandal—before the team would make it to the World Series again.

MIRACULOUS REUNION

The infield of the 1914 Boston Braves—the Miracle Braves who crushed the powerful Philadelphia Athletics in a stunning Series sweep—reunite circa 1925. That's Rabbit Maranville, who was playing for the Cubs at the time, and retired Johnny Evers, Charley Deal, and Butch Schmidt. "Those Braves, they really hurt us," recalled A's manager Connie Mack. "Nobody expected what they did, and it took a long time for us to get over it. Our pride had been shattered."

MUG SHOT

Earl Smith, an itinerant catcher in the 1920s, was oozing feistiness and self-confidence, which shows in this classic portrait. Brought to the majors by John McGraw in 1919, Smith played on the Giants' 1921 and 1922 World Champions, but by mid-1923 the manager had grown sick and tired of his catcher's devotion to arguing and his tendency to solve problems with his fists. "A blankety-blank anarchist!" is what McGraw called Smith as he sent him packing to the Boston Braves, another step on a journey that would take him to Pittsburgh and St. Louis before his career came to an end in 1930.

"AND PLAYING LEFT FIELD..."

As the announcer entertains a sparse crowd, Cleveland Indians player-manager Lou Boudreau (#5) and his Washington Senators counterpart (most likely Bucky Harris or Ossie Bluege) confer with the umpires before a World War II–era game at Washington's Griffith Stadium. Perhaps the two managers were commiserating over the players they'd lost to military service: The Indians were without pitching ace Bob Feller, while the Senators were still reeling from the disappearance of superstar shortstop Cecil Travis.

LADY AND GENTLEMAN

A young fan exchanges a flower for a signed baseball from Connie Mack, grand old man of the Philadelphia Athletics. A's slugger Jimmie Foxx looks on. Fans like this one may have shied away from such fiery managers as John McGraw and Rogers Hornsby, but Mack not only looked and dressed like a gentleman—he *was* one, to players and press and fans alike. For fifty years, as Harold Seymour put it, Mack was "an unforgettable figure, standing at the dugout steps in full view, wearing a dark suit, a tie, and a straw hat or fedora, waving his fielders into position with what became his trademark, a scorecard." The ever-present scorecard is sitting beside Mack on the bench.

THE ORATOR AND THE PEACH

Ty Cobb poses with famous speechmaker, attacker of the theory of evolution, and eternal presidential candidate William Jennings Bryan. Two major-league ballplayers have been named after Bryan: William Jennings Bryan "Pat" Patterson, who got thirty-five at bats in 1921, his sole appearance in the bigs, and William Jennings Bryan "Billy" Herman, Hall of Fame second baseman with the Cubs, Dodgers, and other teams, who finished his fifteen-year career with a .304 batting average. As far as is known, no politician has yet been named after Ty Cobb.

THE THINKER

Johnny Mize, slugger of "tremendous home runs that rang out like the crack of doom" (as Tom Meany and Tommy Holmes put it), in a pensive moment. As was true for many players of his era, Mize's career numbers—359 home runs, 1,337 RBI, a .312 batting average—were slashed by the three prime years he lost serving in the military during World War II. But the Big Cat truly was one of the best hitters of his day, smart at the plate, willing to work out a walk, possessed of power equal to the best of his generation, and fully deserving of his entry into the Hall of Fame.

LOCKED IN

There was never anyone else like Ernie Lombardi, "a huge man, with huge, oak-trunk legs and huge feet and huge hands," as Bill James describes him. "He had huge arms and wrists like giant power cables that snapped around an unnaturally large bat, the heaviest used by any player of his time, and flicked the ball effortlessly wherever he wanted it to go." As if all that wasn't distinctive enough, he was also the only player known to use this interlocking grip on the bat, which he originally adopted to protect an injured finger. Lombardi hit over .300 ten times in his career (1931–47), and the only reason he didn't do even better was that he was so slow the infielders could play in the short outfield, knock down his slashing grounders and line drives, and still throw him out at first.

THE FOURTH MARX BROTHER?

Tinker and Evers and Chance—no, Groucho and Chico and Harpo—
pose with Lou Gehrig in a photograph taken circa 1933, when both
Gehrig (who hit only thirty-two home runs) and the Brothers (who
suffered a major box-office flop with their brilliant *Duck Soup*) had
indifferent years. The Marxes never showed much interest in baseball,
despite using it to disrupt a performance of *Il Trovatore* in their soon-to-
come smash *A Night at the Opera*. Perhaps that explains the opinion
being expressed by Groucho's left hand.

STILL HUSTLING

Even old and overweight, Babe Ruth still took pride in everything he did—including baserunning. "A person familiar with Ruth only through photographs and records could hardly be blamed for assuming that he was a blubbery freak whose ability to hit balls across county lines was all that kept him in the big leagues," wrote the columnist Red Smith. "The truth is he was the complete ballplayer, certainly one of the greatest and maybe the best of all time."

NUMBER FOUR

Milton Berle stops by the locker room to congratulate Sandy Koufax on his fourth no-hitter, a perfect game against the Chicago Cubs in September 1965. That was the season that Koufax, prey all his career to arm injuries, pitched 335 innings and went 26–8. Like most teams at the time, the Dodgers weren't interested in protecting Koufax's long-term health; they wanted him to win as many games as possible right away. "Now, of course, that approach is unthinkable," Bill James comments in the *New Historical Baseball Abstract*. "He'd come out of the game after six, seven innings, they'd push his start back if his elbow swelled up, and he'd go on the DL when it really started to hurt. He'd wind up the year 16–5 rather than 26–7, but he'd pitch until he was forty, rather than being forced into retirement at thirty."

ROWDY RICHARD

"Belligerent [Dick] Bartell is probably the most-hated gent in the National League," wrote Stanley Frank in the *New York Post*. "The boys don't like his flip tongue, his overweening arrogance, and the manner in which he throws his spikes in people's faces while sliding into bases and charging across second on double plays." Opposing players, fans, even his teammates lined up to voice their dislike of the relentlessly intense, argumentative, irascible Rowdy Richard. In this 1931 photograph Bartell (on top), 5'9" and 160 pounds, tussles with his Philly teammate Buzz Arlett, 6'2" and 210.

RHUBARB!

The ever-noisy Dizzy Dean (center, with only his head, including open mouth, showing) and his St. Louis teammates protest a call they didn't like. Such behavior was typical of Dean, Pepper Martin, Joe Medwick, and the other Cardinals immortalized as the Gashouse Gang. "If there were one more like him in baseball, I'd quit the game," said Cardinals executive Branch Rickey of Dean. Added the great pitcher (and outsize personality himself) Burleigh Grimes: "Diz never changed even when he got famous. He was loud and cocky right from the start."

THE PERFECT BENCH JOCKEY

Chicago Cubs' skipper Gabby Hartnett (left) gets outgabbed by Charlie "Dummy" McCarthy and his handler, Edgar Bergen. One of the few characters able to get under W. C. Fields' skin, McCarthy must have found the garrulous Gabby easy prey. What Charlie and Edgar were doing on the field remains unexplained.

THE ROOKIE

All the drive and intensity that Hank Greenberg harnessed his whole career is on display in this 1930 photograph, taken the year Greenberg signed with the Detroit Tigers as a nineteen year old. Greenberg had only one at bat that season, and didn't join the team again until 1933, when he started a streak of eight straight years of hitting over .300 with prodigious power. "It is legend how Hank Greenberg was a self-made ball player—how he would hit until his hands bled and how he would chase after the ball until he was exhausted," wrote Joe Falls.

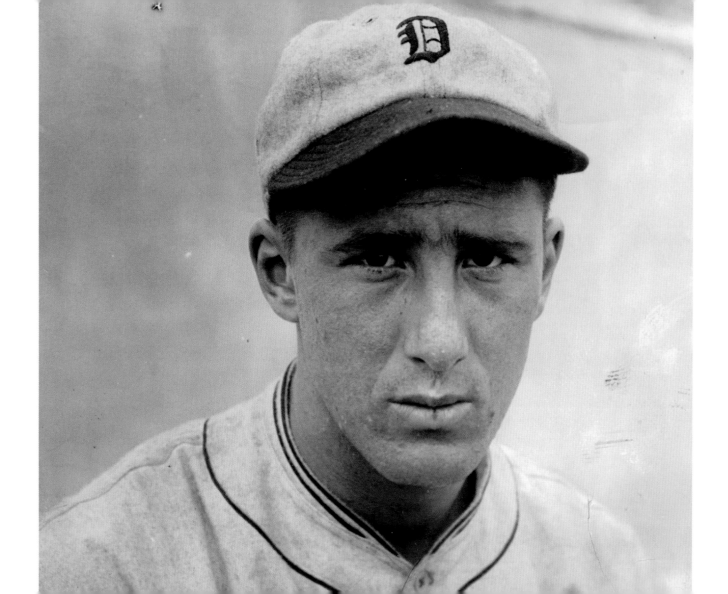

PINCH OF PEPPER

Pepper Martin explodes past first base, safe once again. The defining image of the great, rowdy Cardinals teams of the 1930s, Martin consistently hit around .300, legged out doubles and triples, and scored masses of runs. St. Louis sportswriter Warren Brown said that Martin, with his unorthodox on-field demeanor and grubby uniform, acted like a lightheaded refugee from a gasworks. Thus came the Cards' immortal nickname of that era: the Gashouse Gang.

YESSIR, MR. CAPONE

Chicago Cubs manager Gabby Hartnett signs an autograph for Al Capone. Capone, whose most notorious connection to baseball was his reported use of a bat against those he thought had betrayed him, requested the signed ball for his son (center). The story goes that baseball czar Judge Kenesaw Mountain Landis, hearing about the incident, ordered Hartnett not to sign anything else for Scarface. "Judge, if that's your rule, it's okay by me," Gabby replied. "But I'm not explaining it to him. Next time you see him, *you* explain it to him."

GREAT HITTER, SO-SO MANAGER

Mel Ott uncoils. As a slugger for the New York Giants, and then as the team's manager, Ott was perhaps the most popular of all the Giants from the 1920s through the 1940s. It was the far less likable Leo Durocher—coming over from the despised Brooklyn Dodgers, no less— who had the misfortune of following him as Giants manager. "You can imagine how the Giant fans felt," Durocher wrote in *Nice Guys Finish Last*. "They hated the sight of me; they hated my guts. Durocher, their most despised enemy, in place of Mel Ott, their greatest idol? They like to booed me out of the park."

BUCK'S GLORY

Short and slightly built, but possessing extraordinary power, first baseman Buck Leonard was in his element on the baseball field in Washington's Griffith Stadium. This photo was taken in 1938, nine years before Jackie Robinson broke the color line. At this time, the only opportunity Leonard and many other Negro League stars had to compare themselves to white stars was during occasional exhibition games. "We won our share of the games," he told writer Anthony J. Connor. "We played hard all the time because we wanted to win. It was a matter of pride."

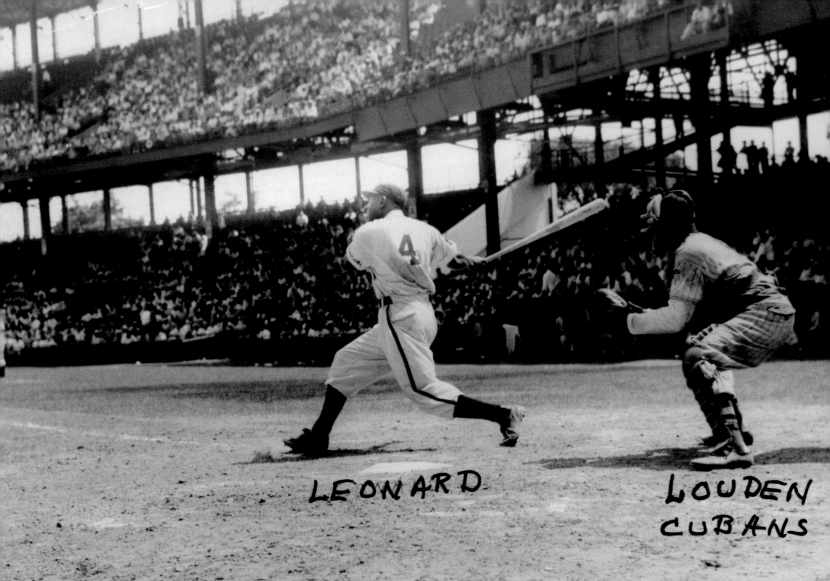

LEONARD

LOUDEN
CUBANS

STRONGMAN

"Let me get a good grip on the bat, as if I wanted to leave my finger-prints on the wood: let me swing with a quick snap which comes from a powerful wrist, and, if I've gotten back of the ball, it sure will travel," said Jimmie Foxx. This approach—and his skills—led to a lifetime total of 534 home runs. In 1932 he slugged fifty-eight homers, at the time the closest anyone had ever come to Babe Ruth's record sixty.

SHINING STARS

Phil Rizzuto and Joe DiMaggio take it easy during batting practice in 1941. DiMaggio was already an established star by then—it was the year of his fifty-six-game hitting streak—but Rizzuto was just a rookie. He had a great first season, hitting .307, followed by an equally strong sophomore season—and then it was off to the Navy for three whole seasons, after which it took him years to get back to where he'd been.

TOO MUCH SLUGGING

Chuck Klein, power-hitting Philadelphia outfielder, was perhaps too powerful for notoriously tight-fisted Phillies owner William F. Baker. According to Fred Lieb, when Klein began hitting home runs in clusters in 1929, "Baker ordered an additional screen of twenty feet added to the screen which already stood atop the right field fence at Baker Bowl. Baker professed his abhorrence for 'cheap home runs' and said that if Chuck Klein wanted to enter the wholesale home run market he should *earn* his homers. Klein suggested the cheapness was on the other side, that Baker didn't want a fifty-home-run player on his team because of the salary he would have to be paid." Klein hit 180 homers from 1929 to 1933. This may have been too many, for he was then traded to the Cubs.

UP THE CREEK

The St. Louis Cardinals' Pepper Martin (left), an unidentified teammate (right), and who—a sumo wrestler?—clown around before a game. Martin had a short career for a star (he played in fewer than 1,200 games), rarely came near to leading the league in any category other than stolen bases, and was no great shakes defensively. But he possessed all the ingredients you needed to be a great baseball story: an irrepressible personality, a way with words, and a gift for coming up with a big hit when people would notice it. Most important of all, he dominated two Cardinals World Series championships, hitting .418 with seven stolen bases in 1931 and 1934 and helping stamp both teams with a wild, unpredictable charm that is remembered fondly today.

FEARLESS LEADER

The peerlessly talented and tough catcher Mickey Cochrane helped lead both the Philadelphia Athletics and (as a player-manager) the Detroit Tigers to World Championships in the 1920s and 1930s. "Mickey Cochrane had a way of reaching men's minds, bodies, and souls," said sportswriter Joe Falls. Like many catchers, he also had the gift of fearlessly trusting his own instincts, making snap decisions that almost always seemed to work out during his peak seasons.

GAVVY, DODE, AND POSSUM

These three men—Gavvy Cravath, Dode Paskert, and Possum Whitted—
helped carry the ordinarily mediocre Philadelphia Phillies to the
National League pennant in 1915. (Cravath, the best player of the three,
led the league with twenty-four home runs and 115 RBI.) As so often
happens to miracle teams, however, cold reality set in once the World
Series began. Facing the overpowering pitching troika of the Boston
Red Sox' Rube Foster, Ernie Shore, and Dutch Leonard, Cravath, Paskert,
and Whitted went a combined six for fifty with 2 RBI as the Phillies
fell in five low-scoring games.

RED, BILL, AND FRANK HANCOCK

An eternal pregame ritual. The stoical Yankees pictured here are veteran third baseman Red Rolfe, Hall of Fame catcher Bill Dickey, and sparkplug shortstop Frank Crosetti. The year is 1939, when the Yankees went 106–45 and rolled over the punchless Cincinnati Reds to win the World Series in four straight. If you could get close enough, you might be able to see other names on the signed balls: Joe DiMaggio, Red Ruffing, perhaps even Lou Gehrig, in this, the season that saw the end of his consecutive-game streak and career.

ANOTHER SIDE OF THE BABE

When we imagine Babe Ruth as a Yankee, we see a big guy with a bat in his hands. But despite his ever-increasing bulk, he always played a smart, aggressive right field, as Charlie Gehringer recalled vividly decades later. "The thing is, he was a darn good fielder," Gehringer told Joe Falls. "He must have bought [his glove] in a drugstore. If you went to Cooperstown to see it, you wouldn't believe it. You wouldn't believe that anybody could catch even one ball with it. But he made great plays and, being a pitcher, he also had a great arm."

LOADED FOR BEAR

Ready to face the firing squad? That's how teams often felt when they came up against the rambunctious St. Louis Cardinals, popularly known as the Gashouse Gang. Here, along with second-string catcher Don Padgett (left) are four of the Gang's leading stars: Joe Medwick, Enos Slaughter, Johnny Mize, and Pepper Martin. But the Gang wasn't quite good enough in 1939, when this photograph was taken: The Cards won ninety-two games but finished behind the Cincinnati Reds in the pennant race.

GET OFF THE FIELD!

His Chicago White Sox players pull forty-four-year-old manager Jimmy Dykes off the field before a game in May 1941. The photo op publicized Dykes' reluctant decision to retire as an active player after nearly a quarter of a century with the White Sox and Philadelphia Athletics. In reality, though, Dykes hadn't had more than a single at bat in a season since 1938, and he hadn't played a full season since 1936. Still, the announcement did make for a good picture.

NECESSARY EVIL

Even a bona fide slugger like Mel Ott (left) had to learn the other skills of the game—including aggressive baserunning. Still, for a player like Ott, the fame, the publicity, and the money all centered on one skill: his ability to hit a baseball. And in that facet of the game, he was one of the best ever, smashing 511 home runs and amassing 1,860 RBI. It was his bat, not his feet, that got him into the Hall of Fame.

SMOOTHEST OF THEM ALL

Some superstars sneak up on the major leagues, while others burst over the game like supernovas. Joe DiMaggio was one of those supernovas, a player whose reputation for brilliance with the San Francisco Seals preceded him to New York. Even as a rookie, he drew large crowds throughout the American League circuit and was given one party after another by Italian-American fans. Yankees executive Edward Barrow warned the young DiMaggio not to get a swelled head, to which the ever-unflappable Yankee Clipper replied: "Don't worry about me, Mr. Barrow. I never get excited."

PINSTRIPED STATUE

Phil Rizzuto demonstrates...well, *something*...in this odd photograph taken in 1955. By then Rizzuto was nearing the end of his career: In 1955 he would bat only 143 times, with a final fifty-two at bats in 1956. Just 5'6" and 160 pounds, Rizzuto was one of the smallest men in his generation to play major-league ball—which made his Hall of Fame career even more impressive. When Casey Stengel, then manager of the Brooklyn Dodgers, first saw Rizzuto, he sent the diminutive short-stop home. Rizzuto shrugged it off, saying, "Casey wasn't the only guy who didn't think I could make it."

LUSCIOUS LUKE

Take a quick glance at Luscious Luke Easter's record with the Cleveland Indians, and you'll see someone whose career peaked early and faded fast. In 1950, his first full year, Easter clubbed twenty-eight home runs and drove in 107. He followed this up with two more seasons that were just as good—but then his major-league stint was suddenly, surprisingly over. But take a closer look: By the end of 1950, his "rookie" year, Luke Easter was already thirty-five years old. Where had he been before that? In the Negro League, of course, pounding the ball. And where did he go after he left the Indians? To the minors, where he kept pounding the ball when he was forty, forty-five, and even forty-seven years old.

AMERICAN IDOL

In August 1942 *Spot Magazine* did a feature on Josh Gibson, the magnificent Negro League catcher. This photograph is especially poignant, for the obvious admiration and affection expressed by the fans, and for the thirty-year-old Gibson's shy pleasure in receiving it. Who knows what Gibson could have done in the major leagues, if only he'd been allowed to try? Who knows if he would have rested easier, been happier, lived longer if he had been given the opportunity to be the idol of everyone, not just his race? As it was, Gibson died only five years after this photograph was taken, leaving only memories, a few photographs, and a plaque in Cooperstown to commemorate his astonishing ability.

SO CLOSE

By 1943, when this photograph was taken, the breaking of the color barrier was just four years away. African Americans were already fighting and dying in the war overseas, and the justification for keeping them out of major-league baseball was growing flimsier by the day. But for Buck Leonard, shown here scoring after hitting a home run in Newark's Ruppert Stadium, four years might as well have been a hundred. He was forty when Jackie Robinson broke the barrier. "I guess they thought about bringing me up at that time, but I was too old," Leonard told Anthony J. Connor. "Cool Papa Bell, Satchel, and me—it was too late for us."

WOMEN ATHLETES:
THREAT OR MENACE?

The All-American Girls Professional Baseball League (AAGPBL) was a booming success from 1943 to 1954. But the whole concept of women participating in sports remained a touchy subject, and even the biggest of big names weighed in. In 1954 "Jimmy Jemail's HOTBOX," a column in *Sports Illustrated*, asked, "Do competitive sports tend to make women less feminine?" Among the responders was a blond actress identified as "Marilyn DiMaggio," who said, "Well, these women champions are very strong. I've always envied them their nice muscles. My husband smiles when I express my admiration for these women. Then he adds: 'Would a man rather take a lovely bit of femininity in his arms or a bundle of muscles?' I'm perplexed. I don't know."

ROBINSON'S REFUGE

Jackie Robinson about to unleash his dangerous swing. "For Jack, the greatest struggles were internal; the pact he had agreed to with Branch Rickey at his signing—that he would not allow himself to be provoked regardless of the viciousness of the baiting—had to be honored," recalled his widow, Rachel. How did he survive? As this photograph shows, he took refuge in the game itself, focusing all his anger and frustration on the ball.

WHERE'S YOUR SEEING-EYE DOG, UMP!?

Yankees fans question a call in a late-season game in 1947, but the kids keep a tight grip on their pop bottles. Over the years, unfortunately, too many fans didn't have as much self-control as these children did. As Leo Durocher recalled, in the seventh game of the 1934 World Series, Tigers fans, furious at the Cards' Joe Medwick, "threw everything they could at him. Fruit, vegetables, pop bottles, seat cushions, spare automobile parts." Today, of course, glass bottles aren't allowed inside major-league stadiums, and automobile parts are also discouraged.

QUEENS FOR THE DAY

Before attendees at a sporting event were called "fans," they were commonly known as "bugs." (An early baseball book was called *Around the World with the Baseball Bugs*.) You can see the source of the nickname in this shot, which looks like nothing so much as a swarm of ants invading a picnic. It's actually Ladies' Day at Yankee Stadium in May 1949. Adding to the antlike impression: Nearly every woman attending the game boasted exactly the same hairstyle, and nearly every man wore a white hat with a black band.

RUMBLING IN

Fellowship exists between catchers, but not when a run is at stake. Here Giants catcher Wes Westrum tries to block the plate and field the throw while also bracing himself for the inevitable collision with his Dodgers counterpart, 200-pound Roy Campanella. Campanella scored in this August 1954 game, but Westrum and the Giants got the last laugh, beating the Dodgers for the National League pennant and then sweeping the favored Cleveland Indians in the World Series.

THE MICK

Mickey Mantle raises a cloud of dust as he scores during a September 1957 game against Detroit. This was one of Mantle's finest seasons: He hit .365 with thirty-four home runs, 121 runs scored, and 94 RBI. In October, though, Mickey and the Yankees suffered a rude shock when they lost the World Series to Lew Burdette (a former Yankees prospect) and the Milwaukee Braves in seven games.

FROM HERE TO ETERNITY

A bugaboo for ballplayers: waiting out the endless hours of a rain delay before the game resumes or the umpires call it. These droopy looking folks—the 1953 Yankees—are trying to make the time pass by watching movies in their locker room. No word on what flick they were watching, but odds are it wasn't a sidesplitting comedy or nail-biting suspense thriller.

WAIT TILL THIS YEAR!

What a season 1955 was for the Dodgers! They started off 9–0 and never looked back, dominating the National League and ending the season 98–55. As every New York baseball fan knows, the Bums then marched into the World Series against the hated Yankees, the team that had beaten them in 1941, 1947, 1949, 1952, and 1953. The Dodgers fell behind, two games to none, won the next three, lost Game Six…and then rode a career-making pitching performance by Johnny Podres to bring Brooklyn its first—and only—World Series title.

We Tie Record Twice
1940-1955
9 Straight !!

Carl Spalberg

SECOND-BASE STYLE

The Dodgers' Jim Gilliam makes an effortless force play in this 1956 game against Don Hoak and the Cubs. For Gilliam, who was associated with the Dodgers from 1953 until his death in 1978, baseball was his life. "You might say I was born on a ball field," he said. "I was playing softball at seven, and hard ball on a sandlot semipro team, the Crawfords, when I was fourteen. I never did anything but play ball."

ROGER'S CORNER

Forlorn Washington Senators' right fielder Gene Woodling and rapt Yankee Stadium fans watch Roger Maris' fly ball drop into the seats. The year was 1961, the homer just one of sixty-one Maris would hit that year. As is well known, Yankees fans resented Maris for challenging the record of the great Babe Ruth, and he disliked New York as well. It made 1961 a nightmarish season for him. "I had splitting headaches, I was smoking twice as much as I normally do and the crowds, the tension, the same questions over and over again were driving me out of my mind," he said after the season.

MISERY LOVES COMPANY

The New York Mets' Frank Thomas hustles back to third base, not yet aware that teammate Charlie Neal already occupies the sack. By the time this photograph was taken, on April 29, 1962, Thomas, Neal, manager Casey Stengel, and the rest of the Mets were already learning to take such blunders in stride. Their loss on this day was just one of an epochal 120 they would total in 1962, still the modern-day record for season-long futility. But the fans, dubbed the "New Breed," didn't care—they loved their team anyway.

SO THIS IS PROGRESS?

Why watch a game in color on a wide expanse of green grass when you can stare at some grainy image on a three-inch screen? Then again, the Los Angeles Coliseum was an absurdly spacious old football stadium with seating for more than 90,000 fans—it was a terrible place to watch a baseball game. Maybe this fan who brought her portable television to a 1959 game was the only one in her section with a clue as to what was happening down on the diamond.

FAN FOR LIFE

A young enthusiast roots for the Mets at a 1964 game. Mets fans back then were far more Amazin' than their team, coming out game after game, year after year, to cheer for the saddest collection of has-been and never-gonna-be players ever collected in one place. In *The Summer Game*, Roger Angell described the moment when he first realized that Mets fans were head over heels in love with their team: "[N]ow there arose from all over the park a full, furious, happy shout of 'Let's go, Mets! Let's go, Mets!' There were wild cries of encouragement before every pitch, boos for every called strike.... Nine runs to the bad, doomed, insanely hopeful, they pleaded raucously for the impossible."

EQUIPPED FOR STARDOM

Chicago White Sox cluster around the batting cage to watch Mickey Mantle take his hacks before a 1962 game. Only a few players in every generation have enough charisma to make fans and even other pros stop and watch, and the Mick was one of them. "I never saw a young player who had so much equipment," marveled Joe DiMaggio. Said Mantle, "It gave me goose bumps to know I had that kind of effect on people."

EN GARDE!

Yankees fans brandish their weapons of choice at the team's second annual Bat Day in 1965. Some of these fans could have done better than the players on the team: The Yankees were on the cusp of what would soon be a complete collapse of the formerly dynastic team. In 1965 they would finish 77-85 (their first sub-.500 season in forty years!), the beginning of a stretch of lean years that wouldn't end until the team made it back to the postseason in 1976.

DA-DA-DA-DAH—CHARGE!!!

New York Mets fans got their entertainment where they could in the early 1960s, when there was little to cheer about down on the field. "Can't anybody here play this game?" Casey Stengel famously asked, but it didn't seem to matter. On a cold, rainy day in May 1963, the stands at the Polo Grounds were packed, and fans led by this trumpeter were still happy to let loose with a chorus of "Let's go, Mets!"

STUDENT OF THE GAME

No one ever paid closer attention to the game of baseball than Casey Stengel. No detail was too small or large for him, and he hid a formidable baseball intellect behind the rambling speeches and goofy catchphrases that made him famous. In Casey's first decade as Yankees manager (1949–58), the Bombers won an astounding nine pennants and seven World Series. It was no coincidence, since Casey lived and breathed the game. "For twenty-seven years all I've heard is baseball," complained Stengel's wife, Edna, in 1952. "If just once in a while we had some other topic of conversation around the house. Even a good messy ax murder."

MARVELOUS

One notorious early hero to Mets fans was "Marvelous" Marv Throneberry, who got little more than a cup of coffee with the team, yet came to symbolize its irresistible, if chaotic, spirit. Fans of other teams (especially the Yankees) couldn't understand why the Mets were so beloved, but the writer Jimmy Breslin could. "You see, the Mets are losers, just like nearly everybody else in life," he wrote in *Can't Anybody Here Play This Game*? "This is a team for the cab driver who gets held up and the guy who loses out on a promotion because he didn't maneuver himself to lunch with the boss enough. It is the team for every guy who has to get out of bed in the morning and go to work for short money on a job he does not like."

PEERLESS

Sandy Koufax celebrates his second no-hitter, a 1963 masterpiece against the San Francisco Giants, as manager Walt Alston beams over his right shoulder. All Koufax did in 1963 was go 25–5, with an astounding twenty complete games, eleven shutouts, and 306 strike-outs—and then follow this astonishing season with two complete-game victories in the Dodgers' extermination of the Yankees in the World Series. "A guy who throws what he intends to throw—that's the definition of a good pitcher," Koufax said. For Sandy at career peak, it was goose eggs.

WATCH OUT FOR BLACK CATS

Eddie Collins, who hit .333 and compiled 3,315 hits in a twenty-five-year career (1906–30), danced through the years with style, grace, and fearless intensity. He seemed the most stable of ballplayers, though inside he wasn't free of gremlins. "While I have no fear of Friday the thirteenth, I recognize that July first is a tough day for the Collins family. I have suffered three considerable accidents in baseball and every one of them occurred on July first," he said. "You won't find me slacking on that day, but you may be certain of one thing. I will be well aware what day of the month it is and heartily glad when I can cross that day off the calendar."

TAKING INFIELD

In this odd photograph, Mets ace Tom Seaver appears to be practicing fielding ground balls—not something casual onlookers saw very often. Seaver is confronting the challenge with his usual uncompromising intensity. ("If you don't think baseball is a big deal, don't do it. But if you do it, do it right," he said.) Something—could it be Seaver's demeanor?—seems to be cracking up manager Gil Hodges (rear), usually quite the stoic himself.

CAPTAIN KANGAROO

Court is in session in the Baltimore Orioles' clubhouse, and superstar Frank Robinson is chief judge. (Robinson kept the team's mood light by pronouncing sentences on teammates for various "transgressions"— such as when he levied a fine against Brooks Robinson for showboating during his brilliant 1970 Series.) "Mostly, the Orioles were fun," wrote Tim Kurkjian of Baltimore's championship teams of the 1960s and 1970s. "They were Frank Robinson in a ridiculous wig, presiding over the team's kangaroo court. They were Earl Weaver, all 5'7" of him, cap on backward, stretching on tiptoes to get in the face of an umpire.... They were Rick Dempsey slipping and sliding around the tarp-covered infield in his slap-stick rain-delay routine." The Orioles were fun...and also they won.

LADIES' DAY

It's a tradition that began in the nineteenth century, when teams were desperate to entice women to ballparks that must have seemed like enemy territory: dark and dirty, filled with potentially dangerous men in the stands and on the field alike. Though the Mets didn't need gimmicks to attract fans (male or female) in the early 1960s, they kept the tradition alive, allowing women in on certain dates for a cut-rate price of just fifty cents a ticket. These fans, attending an early season game at the new Shea Stadium in 1964, seem to appreciate the gesture.

PEPPER PLAYING ALLOWED

A group of St. Louis Cardinals warm up before an April 1963 game against the Mets at the Polo Grounds, then in its last season. The two teams were racing full speed in opposite directions. The Cards, just rounding into championship form, would go 93–69 and finish second to the Los Angeles Dodgers, while the second-year Mets would win just fifty-one games. The Cardinals' four top pitchers (Bob Gibson, Ernie Broglio, Curt Simmons, and Ray Sadecki) combined for sixty-one victories, while Al Jackson (13–17) was the only Met in double figures. Unsurprisingly, the Cards went 13–5 against the Mets that season.

BUCKETFOOT AL'S BIG DAY

In what was the first regularly scheduled All-Star Game (billed as "The Game of the Century" by the press), that's the Philadelphia Phillies' Chuck Klein on the right and the Chicago White Sox' Al Simmons on the left. Simmons seems to appear in virtually every photograph taken of the 1933 All-Star Game, for one simple reason: The game was suggested by a Chicago sportswriter, was played in conjunction with the Chicago Exposition, and took place at the Chicago White Sox' Comiskey Park. The White Sox were a poor team in the early 1930s (in 1932 they went 49–102), and they'd just acquired Simmons, a certified star, from the Philadelphia Athletics. Bucketfoot Al was Chicago's horse, and they were going to ride him as far as they could.

LINEUP OF LEGENDS

What an amazing crew the 1933 American League All-Star team was! In this crowd are Lou Gehrig, Babe Ruth, Joe Cronin, Lefty Grove, Bill Dickey, Al Simmons, Lefty Gomez, Eddie Collins, Tony Lazzeri, Jimmie Foxx, Earl Averill, Rick Ferrell, and Charlie Gehringer—a Home Run Baker's dozen of future Hall of Famers. In the game itself one superstar bestrode them all: thirty-eight-year-old Babe Ruth, who slugged a home run and made a spectacular running catch in right field. No one had a sense of timing like the Babe.

VICTIMS OF THE "THING"

Imagine being a National League pitcher having to face Al Simmons, Lou Gehrig, Babe Ruth, and Jimmie Foxx at the 1934 All-Star Game. Well, the New York Giants' great Carl Hubbell confronted exactly that predicament at the start of the game. Pitching carefully, he allowed two men to get on base with none out. But then Gabby Hartnett, the cheerful catcher, came to the mound. "Look, Hub," he said, "never mind all that junk about being careful and pitching this way or that way. Just throw that 'thing.' It'll get 'em out. It always gets me out!" That "thing" was the screwball, and with it he struck out Ruth, Gehrig, and Foxx to get out of the inning. He then whiffed Simmons and Joe Cronin in the second for an All-Star record five Ks in a row—against five future Hall of Famers.

ALL-STAR ALL-TIMER

Throughout his magnificent twenty-three-year career, Hank Aaron (posing here with the Cleveland Indians' Harvey Kuenn before the 1960 All-Star Game at Yankee Stadium) rarely got the ink afforded fellow superstars Mickey Mantle, Willie Mays, Roberto Clemente, and others. But teammates, managers, and fans recognized Aaron's greatness, voting him onto the All-Star team every year from 1955 through 1975. In four of those years (1959–62), the leagues held two All-Star Games, giving Aaron and the others twice as many opportunities to strut their stuff on the national stage.

ALL-STAR SLIDE

Charlie Gehringer makes it to third safely in an action shot from the 1933 All-Star Game, the first ever. The game was notable for many reasons, not the least of which was that it pitted two Hall of Fame managers—the Giants' John McGraw and the Athletics' Connie Mack—against each other. Mack would manage another seventeen seasons (though he'd never win another pennant), but 1933 marked McGraw's first year away from the game since before the century began. Ill health had forced his retirement from the Giants during the 1932 season, but he was called back to manage this one final game—sadly for him, a 4–2 American League victory.

NEW YORK, NEW YORK, NEW YORK

A panoply of Manhattan, Bronx, and Brooklyn stars, circa 1942. That's the Giants' Mel Ott on the left, in his seventeenth major-league season but still only thirty-three years old; the Dodgers' Billy Herman, newly arrived from the Chicago Cubs and soon to leave the game for the military, center; and the Yankees' Bill Dickey, already the veteran of six World Series (and six World Championships) on the right. Of the three teams, only the Yankees would make it to the Series in 1942—and they'd lose to the Cardinals in five games.

SKIPPERS

The three New York managers: the Yankees' Joe McCarthy, the Giants' Mel Ott, and the Dodgers' Leo Durocher in the mid-1940s. It is a baseball truth that great players—especially sluggers—make worse managers than do scrappy middle infielders and career minor leaguers. McCarthy never made it to the majors, but he led the Yankees to eight pennants in fifteen full seasons. Durocher, a career .247 hitter, kept his Dodgers and Giants teams in the pennant race season after season, culminating in the Giants' stunning Series victory in 1954. And Ott? His Giants finished above .500 just three times in his seven-year managerial career.

FORWARD, MARCH!

The Cleveland Indians prepare to defend their ballpark from enemy attack during World War I. According to General John J. Pershing, playing sports made Americans especially apt at the game of war. "The avidity with which American soldiers are entering into the activities of the war on the battle line is astonishing to European armies," he claimed in early 1918. "In the matter of grenade and bomb throwing the Americans become proficient in but a few days' drill. I attribute this in part to the American games, baseball and football."

ALL STARS OF THE SEVEN SEAS

Virginia, Ohio, New Jersey, Vermont, and other states (and the warships named after them) are represented in this rare shot of the All-Fleet Base Ball Team of 1907–08. During World War I, Casey Stengel—a ship painter at the Brooklyn Navy Yard—fielded a local Navy team that played teams from warships coming into port. "We specialized in playing those shipwreck teams," Casey recalled. "Players who had been at sea for three or four months were still seasick. As soon as those ships came in, I jumped on board, got to the athletic officer, and scheduled those games at Prospect Park. I believe you could have a good record that way."

"All Fleet Base Ball Team" 1907 & 8.

Sydney, aus.

ALWAYS ON GUARD

A huge crowd packs Yankee Stadium for Game One of the 1943 World Series, while the scorecard focuses on real-world concerns. Even after dozens of ballplayers left the game to serve in the military, baseball continued to thrive as a patriotic leisure-time activity. "Born in America, propagated in America and recognized as the National Game, baseball and all those engaged in the sport are Americans first, last, and always," opined the editors of *The Sporting News*.

TIME TO BAIL OUT

Appropriately warlike in design, given its unveiling in 1942, this lethal-looking device was actually the first automatic pitching machine. That's the Cleveland Indians' future Hall of Famer Lou Boudreau on the right (with coach George Susce). It's easy for Boudreau to smile: He's standing next to the machine, not cowering at the plate as it fires rock-hard horsehide missiles at him.

WARTIME REWARD

For this August 1944 Sunday game at Brooklyn's Ebbets Field, the stands were packed with schoolchildren who had sold war bonds to raise money for the troops overseas. Fundraising for the war effort was intense in Brooklyn and elsewhere; players roamed the stands before games, selling war bonds, and even Brooklyn general manager Branch Rickey, who never went to games on Sunday, showed up at the ballpark to help celebrate the Dodgers' role in selling $180 million worth in Brooklyn alone.

IN CASE OF AIR RAID
FOLLOW ARROW

A BREAK FROM THE ACTION

Attired in uniforms of very different kinds, a World War I-era fleet team poses for posterity. Washington Senators owner Clark Griffith was a leading force in providing uniforms and other equipment to military personnel. Between 1917 and 1919, Griffith sent more than three thousand kits to the troops, each including catcher's equipment, a first baseman's glove, three bats, three bases, a dozen balls, a dozen scorecards, and a rulebook. Griffith and the rest of the American League even helped keep the struggling *Sporting News* alive when its subscriptions plummeted during the war, buying 150,000 copies and sending them overseas.

BARRACKS BALL

Soldiers relax with a quick game at Camp Gordon, Georgia, in 1918. Back in the major leagues, World War I was having a drastic effect. As soon as the United States entered the war, the leagues came under attack by critics who considered it inappropriate to keep playing a game during wartime. In response to the dwindling gate receipts that accompanied this controversy, the majors shortened the 1918 season to 140 games, ending it on Labor Day. More than 225 ballplayers joined the service, and at least three died in action, though many spent their time leading ball teams in training camps and shipyards in the U.S. and overseas.

NO TANS THIS YEAR

New York Giants manager Mel Ott (in uniform) and members of the New York press huddle together for warmth in Lakewood, New Jersey, circa 1944. During World War II, teams abandoned their southern spring-training sites, opting to train closer to home. The Giants' choice was a nine-hole golf course rebuilt as a ballfield. But the often-bitter conditions didn't bother Ott any, according to outfielder Whitey Lockman. "He was frolicking, and sometimes he was without a sweat-shirt," Lockman recalled. "And, my God, he was from Louisiana."

TWO GENERATIONS IN WARTIME

On the left is Cardinals pitcher Johnny Beazley, who entered the military after going 21–6 in 1942, missed three seasons during World War II, and was never able to re-establish himself after the war ended. He's with former Boston Braves catcher Hank Gowdy, the first major leaguer to enlist during World War I. "The highest honor of my entire life came through being privileged to wear the United States Army uniform and serve my country in the last war in which it was engaged," Gowdy said. In 1943, at the age of fifty-three, he joined up again and was commissioned as an Army captain.

THE FLEET'S IN

A ship's worth of fans watch Navy inductee Johnny Mize at bat in a 1943 game at the Naval Training Center in Great Lakes, Illinois. Many (though certainly not all) baseball stars spent much of their time in the service playing baseball, and the Great Lakes team was the Yankees of military installations. Coached by Mickey Cochrane, the squad included Mize, Bob Feller, Schoolboy Rowe, and Billy Herman. They went 52–10 in 1943 and improved to 48–2 in 1944, a mark that included a 17–3 whupping of the major-league Cleveland Indians.

ESPRIT DE CORPS

A Naval training school team from 1916, at the height of World War I. It's easy to smile at how much time sailors and soldiers seemed to spend playing baseball, but it wouldn't be long before many of these men would be in combat overseas. The familiar game of baseball provided comfort and security in frighteningly uncertain times. As the *New York Times* put it, "Athletic games can do more to establish the desired esprit de corps in an army's organization than anything aside from actual participation in battle."

Naval Training
Season

GREETINGS FROM THE NAVY YARD

Future Hall of Famer Billy Herman (umpiring that day), Red Sox star Johnny Pesky (center), and pals discuss the ground rules prior to a wartime game at the Brooklyn Navy Yard. By 1944, more than two hundred players listed on major-league rosters were in the service, including such stars as Herman, Pesky, Joe DiMaggio, Ted Williams, Hank Greenberg, Cecil Travis, and Bob Feller. Many got the chance to stay in some semblance of physical shape by playing baseball in military training camps, Navy yards, and other facilities for the duration of the war.

SOLDIERS AND SAILORS

A rare shot of military All-Star ballplayers posing in their uniforms during World War II. That's Bob Feller, fifth from left in the center row, with old-timers George Earnshaw, Mickey Cochrane, and Hank Gowdy to his right. Third from the right in the same row is Cecil Travis, a huge star with the Washington Senators in the prewar years but virtually forgotten today. Travis may have been the star whose career was most drastically affected by the war: He hit over .300 eight of his first nine years in the majors, culminating in a spectacular .359 mark with 218 hits in 1941 before signing up. Though he was only thirty-two when he returned in 1945, his skills were gone.

THE VOLUNTEER

Hank Greenberg (left) in full Army regalia. Famously, Greenberg had completed his military obligations just a few days before Pearl Harbor, but re-enlisted as soon as the United States entered the war. "This doubtless means I am finished with baseball, and it would be silly for me to say I do not leave it without a pang," Hank said at the time. "But all of us are confronted with a terrible task—the defense of our country and the fight of our lives." Greenberg was wrong about one thing: After serving bravely, he did return to star in baseball again when the war finally ended.

STARS IN WARTIME

In February 1942, just a few weeks after Pearl Harbor, Hank Greenberg, Joe DiMaggio, and Mel Ott receive honors for their accomplishments of 1941. Greenberg had already rejoined the Army, and DiMaggio was soon to hang up his spikes and head off to service as well. Ott, player-manager of the New York Giants, stayed home to witness the oft-comical hijinks that characterized wartime major-league baseball, when teenagers, one-armed men, and almost anyone else who knew how to swing a bat and wear a glove were welcomed into the majors.

FELLER'S FELLOWS

Bob Feller (front row, third from right), and his powerful Navy team pose in May 1944. By this time Feller, still only twenty-five, had already missed two full seasons of his career with the Cleveland Indians. He wouldn't return to the club until late 1945, and though he'd remain a great pitcher for another five years, he—like so many others—missed what likely would have been his finest seasons. Even so, his 266 wins and 2,581 career strikeouts earned him quick entry into the Hall of Fame.

IT HAPPENED IN BROOKLYN

During World War II, all entertainment industries worked together to raise both money and morale among those fighting overseas and back home. Here, Frank Sinatra belts out a tune with Dodgers coach Chuck Dressen and assorted onlookers, in a 1944 photograph taken at Ebbets Field. (Wonder if they were singing "Take Me Out to the Ball Game," the title of a movie Sinatra would make five years later?) One question: Since Dodgers manager Leo Durocher never missed a chance to share the limelight, where was he when Frank showed up?

KEEPING GOING

During World War II, even American prisoners of war kept their sanity by forming teams and playing baseball. (Uniforms and equipment were supplied by the Red Cross and other relief agencies.) This is the team at German Stalag 111B in 1944, still months away from rescue and release by the Allied forces. In his semiautobiographical 2004 novel *Double Play*, set during and after the war, mystery writer Robert Parker captures what baseball meant back then. It was, he wrote, "like the sound of a mother's heartbeat to her unborn child, the rhythm of life and certainty. The sound of permanence."

DON'T ASK WHERE

The caption of this U.S. Marine Corps photograph identifies the batter as PFC Robert Hogan of Waterloo, Illinois, the catcher as Corporal Joseph Hargreves of Saylesville, Rhode Island, and the umpire as Sergeant Stanley R. Merrill of Redlands, California. But the location of this well-attended World War II game was a carefully guarded secret, to be kept at all costs from the Japanese. So these soldiers were said to be on an "island in the South Pacific," not much of a revelation, given the abundance of palm trees in the background.

BOMBS BURSTING IN AIR

No, this remarkable photograph doesn't show a group of lunatic soldiers playing a ballgame in the heat of a battle. But the reality was dramatic enough: These members of the United States Army Signal Corps found room for a diamond right beside an artillery range. The flying dirt, the weapons and helmets leaning against the fence in the foreground, the focus and intensity of the players—all this demonstrates the importance of baseball as a relief, a tonic, a lifeline for soldiers far from home and facing an uncertain future.

THE WEDDING BELLS PLAYED "REVEILLE"

Like scores of his fellow ballplayers, Early Wynn (center) lost time from his career to serve in the military during World War II. In September 1944, however, he focused on another off-the-field activity: getting married. Here, Early and his bride, Lorraine, prepare to exchange vows before a U.S. Army chaplain. They would be married for half a century, and Early established a reputation as one of the toughest hurlers ever, willing to knock down anybody at any time. When asked if he would throw at his own mother, he supposedly replied, "I would if she were crowding the plate."

HAUTE CUISINE

Ted Williams ingests a local delicacy—a live clam—offered to him by the South Korean woman who dove to obtain it. After losing three full seasons to World War II, Williams (who described himself as a "nearly deaf, pneumonia-prone, thirty-four-year-old pilot with a bum elbow") was angry to be called back to service during the Korean War. "I wasn't crazy about it, no way," he said in *My Life in Pictures*. "In fact, deep down I was damn bitter about it—but I went."

THE COSTS OF WAR

Many ballplayers lost three or four years of their careers to World War II. Countless thousands of soldiers lost their lives. But the war's toll even on those too young to fight is hinted at in this 1944 picture, featuring Ted Williams at the left. The little girl is Patricia Ann Lewis, three and a half, born at Pearl Harbor just before the Japanese attack and evacuated with her mother soon after. Her father, Chief Parachute Rigger J. C. Lewis (not pictured), was wounded in fighting in the Pacific, but survived. To Patricia Ann—a huge fan of Williams—as to so many others, attending a ballgame was a sign that some things could still be depended on.

OFF WITH ONE UNIFORM, ON WITH ANOTHER

Looking back, it seems like Ted Williams never got a break with the fans or the press. The sole support of his mother, Williams received a deferment from the military after Pearl Harbor. When the deferment was revoked, he appealed and had it reinstated. "But, what a howl!" he recalled of the public's reaction. "You'd have thought Teddy Ballgame had bombed Pearl Harbor himself. Unpatriotic. Yellow. Those were some of the *milder* epithets." In the face of such public scorn, Williams signed up with the Marines, training as a pilot—and then went on to serve again during the Korean War.

SOLEMN VOW

Willie Mays enters the Army on May 28, 1952. Only a handful of players missed significant time from the game during the Korean War, but Mays—who had just turned twenty-one—was one of them. He spent most of 1952 and all of 1953 in the service, and returned in 1954. "I rushed over and gave him such a hug that I almost put him out of commission," Giants manager Leo Durocher recalled of seeing the prodigal Mays return. Leo's enthusiasm made all sorts of sense: In 1954 Mays hit .345, slugged forty-one homers, won the N.L. Most Valuable Player Award, and led the Giants to a World Series championship.

TWO KINDS OF SUPERSTAR

Look at the expressions on the faces of these 1953 Brooklyn Dodgers—
Clem Labine, Carl Erskine, Jackie Robinson, and Preacher Roe—and
you'll see respect, affection, humility, even awe. The story behind the
photo tells why: The men on the other side of the food line (left to
right, Sergeant Wesley Murra of Manhattan and Sergeant Pedro Pereira
and Corporal Leonard Chiarelli of Brooklyn) were recently returned
prisoners of war from Korea. Their bravery and sacrifice had earned
the respect of the Dodgers stars—as well as this hearty meal.

START SPREADING THE WORD

Dizzy Dean and the rest of the eternally cocky St. Louis Cardinals of 1934 (that's a grinning Dean second from the right) pose with the Grunow World Cruiser, the only radio with "the amazing Signal Beacon." Diz and the Cards certainly made enough radio-worthy news in 1934, winning ninety-five games and the National League pennant, and then going on to defeat the Detroit Tigers in a thrilling World Series. The Gashouse Gang was larger than life: Dean never stopped talking, Joe Medwick never stopped glowering, Pepper Martin pulled stunts like rifle-hunting birds at 70 mph from the team bus, and player-manager Frank Frisch barely maintained his sanity.

ONLY
Grunow Radio
"WORLD
CRUISER"

has the amazing SIGNAL BEACON
STOPS YOU AT THE STATIONS OF THE WORLD

GRUNOW
ELECTRIC RECEIVER

MODEL No. 550
GRUNOW
ELECTRIC RECEIVER

GRUNOW
ELECTRIC RECEIVER

ST. LOUIS CARDINALS
1934

MEDWICK · GONZALES CRAWFORD WHITEHEAD MOONEY MARTIN VANCE P. DEAN FRISCH HAINES HALLAHAN DUROCHER ROTHROCK J. DEAN PIPPE
HALEY WALKER DELANCEY ORSATTI CARLETON FULLIS DAVIS COLLINS WARES

WHERE IT ALL BEGAN

Fans flock to Boston's Huntington Avenue Grounds for a 1903 World Series game—the first-ever championship series between the long-established National League and the upstart American League, finishing just its third season. The Series pitted the Boston Americans (later the Red Sox) against Honus Wagner's heavily favored Pittsburgh Pirates. But Wagner was battling injuries, the madly enthusiastic Boston fans rattled the Pirates, the Americans' Bill Dineen won three games, and Boston won the best-of-nine Series, five games to three. If anyone had doubted it previously, it was now clear that the American League deserved its place on the big stage.

EMERSON
SHOE
GOODYEAR
WELT
$3.50
HAND
SEWED
HUNTINGT
AVENUE
AMERICAN LEAGUE
BASE BA
GROUNDS

MOMENTARY JOY

Team leader Gabby Hartnett (left), Tex Carleton (right), and other Chicago Cubs celebrate the 1935 season, which saw the Cubs win 100 games and nip the great St. Louis Cardinals for the National League pennant. Led by Hartnett, Billy Herman, and such wandering stars as Rogers Hornsby and Hack Wilson, the Cubs were a darn good team in the 1930s, winning ninety-plus games four times and capturing three pennants. Unfortunately, they bombed in the World Series, losing to the Tigers, four games to two, in 1935 and being absolutely flattened by the Yankees in a pair of four-game sweeps in 1932 and 1938.

SWEEP CITY

Could any team look happier or more relaxed than the Yankees do in this September 1928 team picture? The Bombers, coming off their four-game dismantling of the Pittsburgh Pirates in the 1927 World Series, had just concluded a season in which they won 101 games and the A.L. pennant. They sure don't look overawed by their 1928 Series opponent, the St. Louis Cardinals. Remarkably, due to several Yankees injuries, some pundits actually expected the Cards to win. But Lou Gehrig hit four home runs and drove in nine, Babe Ruth went ten for sixteen with three homers, and the Yanks completed an effortless sweep. That's Ruth grinning in the back row on the far left, Gehrig on the far right, and joyful manager Miller Huggins in the dark suit, center.

NEW YORK YANKEES 1928

FACING DEFEAT

Even before the 1907 World Series begins, the Detroit Tigers look tense and unhappy. A superb team that took on the persona of its tormented star, Ty Cobb (middle row, third from left), the Tigers won three straight A.L. pennants from 1907 to 1909. But Cobb and his team knew nothing but misery in the Series, getting swept by the Chicago Cubs in 1907, losing to the Cubs again in 1908, and falling to Honus Wagner's Pittsburgh Pirates in seven games in 1909, with Cobb hitting .231 in his last Series appearance. "I have often wished that when I was at the peak of my playing skill in my late twenties or early thirties, I had had another crack at a World Series," Cobb told writer Fred Lieb years later. "I'm sure I would have done better."

FAMILIAR SIGHT

Joe DiMaggio (back row, second from left) and his Yankees teammates celebrate the news that they have clinched the A.L. pennant on September 15, 1947. The Yankees went on to finish a yawn-inducing twelve games in front of their nearest challenger (the Detroit Tigers) and marched into the World Series a confident team. But their N.L. opponents, the Brooklyn Dodgers, gave the Yankees all they could handle. It was a classic Series, featuring Jackie Robinson's first post-season appearance, Bill Bevens' near no-hitter, Al Gionfriddo's famous catch against DiMaggio, and other unforgettable moments. In the end, though, the Yankees prevailed, as they nearly always did.

BOARD'S-EYE VIEW

It wasn't exactly a front-row seat, but Jeff Ingenito didn't care. Ingenito was the "Yanks' number-one knothole fan," as the newspapers put it: the scoreboard attendant at Yankee Stadium. He watched the action through a little window in the scoreboard and then, using an ingenious system of pulleys and weights, posted the score. On the day this photo was taken—October 6, 1949—Ingenito didn't have much work to do: The Brooklyn Dodgers edged the Yankees, 1–0, behind Preacher Roe, in the second game of the World Series. After that, the Series moved to Ebbets Field, where the Yankees wrapped up a five-game victory under the watchful eye of the Dodgers' unheralded scoreboard attendant.

THANKS FROM ALL TRUE FANS

Despite boasting superstar player-manager Tris Speaker (front row between the two men in suits), the 1920 Cleveland Indians are not the best-remembered championship team of their era. At the time, though, they were considered a godsend, for they edged the Chicago White Sox by two games for the 1920 A.L. pennant. Late in the season, the 1919 Black Sox scandal had finally unraveled and Joe Jackson and other Sox stars had been suspended. It would have been a nightmare to see the depleted, scandal-ridden Sox stumble onto the field to face the Brooklyn Robins in the World Series. Instead, Speaker led the Indians to a tidy—and above all, clean—victory over the Robins, earning the gratitude of baseball fans nationwide.

©by L.Van Oeyen.Cleveland.O.

(Middle Row)—Chester D. Thomas, c., J. Gladstone Graney, o.f., Guy Morton, p., James C. Bagby, p.,
Ray Caldwell, p., Leslie Nunamaker, c., Geo. J. Burns, 1st b., R. W. Clark, p., S. F. O'Neill, c.,
W. Lawrence Gardner, 3rd b., Odenwald, sub.

w.—Left to Right) Jack McCallister, Coach., J. P. Evans, o.f., Charles D. Jamieson, o.f.,
Johnston, 1st b., James C. Dunn, Pres., Tris Speaker, Mgr. and o.f., Walter McNichols, Sec.,
Elmer J. Smith, o.f., Stanley Coveleskie, p., Joseph Sewell, s.s.

(Back Row)—J. Walter Mails, p., Cykowski, sub., Hamilton, sub., Geo. E. Uhle, p., Joe Wood
William Wambsganss, 2nd b., Harry Lunte, i.f., Smallwood, Trainer. (Upper Corner) Ray Cha

CLEVELAND AMERICAN LEAGUE BASE BALL CLUB
CHAMPIONS 1920

THE MASTER

Some called him Bob, others Mose, but today he's almost always referred to as Lefty. Robert Moses Grove was already twenty-five and an acknowledged star when he left the powerful minor-league Baltimore Orioles in 1925 to join the Philadelphia Athletics. He then unleashed his terrifying fastball and devastating curve upon American League hitters for seventeen more years, winning twenty-plus games eight times and leading the Athletics to three pennants and two Series victories. As a child, Grove played baseball with a cork wrapped in an old sock and covered with black tape. "I also got fast throwing rocks," he said. "We'd throw rocks at anything, moving or stationary."

TWO YEARS LATER, SANTA BROUGHT BABE RUTH

This charming portrait shows Chicago Cubs' star pitcher Charlie Root with his family at Christmas in 1930. Root was a fine pitcher with the Cubs, good enough to win 201 games in a seventeen-year career. Today, however, he is best remembered for being the man on the mound when Babe Ruth "pointed" toward the center-field fence before homering during the 1932 World Series. But that wasn't Root's only brush with infamy. During Game Four of the 1929 Series, he held an 8–0 lead over the Philadelphia Athletics—only to surrender the first six runs of what turned into a ten-run inning for the A's as they stormed to victory. Here's hoping his beautiful family gave him surcease from his World Series nightmares on the mound.

SITTING DUCKS

The tough-guy Chicago Cubs line up after winning the National League pennant in 1932. The Cubs were not only a fine ballclub, they were past masters at the art of bench-jockeying. And who better to jockey than the New York Yankees, their opponents in the World Series that year, in particular Babe Ruth? It was the catcalls from the Cubs' bench—especially Guy Bush (front row, second from right)—that provoked Ruth into supposedly pointing towards the center-field stands before slamming a home run in Game Three of the Yankees' four-game sweep. According to Lou Gehrig, Ruth merely flapped his hand at the Cubs. "The gestures were meant for Bush," Gehrig recalled. "Ruth was going to foul one into the dugout, but when the pitch came up, big and fat, he belted it."

STAY WITHIN THE LINES!

Young field attendants paint home plate as umpires consult with the
New York Giants and Philadelphia Athletics prior to a 1911 World Series
game at New York's Polo Grounds. Unfortunately for the home team,
the A's left their footprints on the plate during the Series more than
twice as often as the Giants, establishing a depressing trend for New
York in the 1910s (four Series appearances, no championships). In 1911,
the A's rode to a six-game triumph behind the superb pitching of
Chief Bender, Jack Coombs, and Eddie Plank.

THE INFANT BABE

Can you spot Babe Ruth in this team photo of the World Champion 1915 Red Sox? There he is in the back row, still just a green pea, grinning like he can't believe his outrageously good fortune. But Babe seemed to have been born with baseball smarts. In 1915, when he was just twenty years old, he went 18–8 with a 2.44 ERA, the first of three spectacular seasons as a pitcher before his manager decided, for some reason, that he was better employed with an outfielder's glove and a bat in his hands. His final regular-season numbers as a Sox pitcher: 89–46, with seventeen shutouts.

MESSAGE FROM ABOVE

A blizzard of leaflets interrupts play at Yankee Stadium during the fourth inning of Game Six of the 1957 Series between the Yanks and Milwaukee Braves. The leaflets urged fans (and Braves' coach Connie Ryan) to support Fidel Castro in his ongoing battle to overthrow Cuban ruler Fulgencio Batista. Fidel was, by all accounts, an avid fan of the game and a passable pitcher himself. Who knows? If only he'd possessed a better fastball or sharper-breaking curve, by 1957 he might have found himself pitching baseballs instead of revolution.

FANS GREW IN BROOKLYN

All ages, races, and genders were welcome in the most egalitarian plane t in the solar system: Brooklyn, New York, home to the Dodgers and their irrepressible fans. Who else would have put up with heart-breaking losses to their hated rivals, the Yankees, in 1941, 1947, 1949, 1952, and 1953, before finally reaching the promised land in 1955? This photo, of fans waiting for bleacher-seat tickets to go on sale, was taken prior to the first game of the 1952 Series, a seven-game thriller in which the Yankees trailed, three games to two, before winning two nailbiters to capture their fourth World Series in a row. For these Dodgers rooters, it was "Wait Till Next Year!"...again.

THE DYNASTY BEGINS

The 1906 Chicago Cubs pose for a rather absent-minded team photograph after capturing the N.L. pennant with a 116–36 record. Led by
Three Finger Brown and the all-time infield of Tinker, Evers, and
Chance, the Cubs were heavy favorites over the Chicago White Sox,
the famed "Hitless Wonders." In the Series, however, the Sox outscored
the Cubs 22–18 and captured the championship in six games. But the
Cubs were not to be denied, coming back to win the pennant—and
the World Series—in both 1907 and 1908.

1 2 3 4 5 6

7 8 9 10 11 12 13

14 15 16 17 18

KID
HERMAN

PYRIGHT 1906
FRED H. WAGNER

ESTER (2) LUNDGREN (3) BROWN (4) SHECKARD (5) KLING (6) TAYLOR (7) SHULTE (8) HOFMAN (9) STEINFELDT
HANCE (11) OVERALL (12) EVERS (13) SLAGLE (14) MORAN (15) GESSLER (16) WALSH (17) McCORMICK (18) TINK

LOOK! WE'RE IN HERE!

Whitey Ford and Yogi Berra check out some World Series stats. They undoubtedly liked what they saw: Whitey's Series marks included twenty-two starts and ten wins (both the most ever), a 2.71 ERA, and three shutouts. Yogi's numbers are even more impressive: a record fourteen Series appearances, 259 at bats, seventy-one hits, and ten doubles, along with twelve home runs, forty-one runs scored, and 39 RBI. Perhaps most importantly, Ford contributed to six World Series championships, Berra to an astounding ten. Of course, it didn't hurt to have Mickey Mantle, Phil Rizzuto, Roger Maris, and other stars on the team as well.

A TRIUMPHANT GRIN

Babe Ruth and Lou Gehrig celebrate Ruth's famous "called shot" home run. While Gehrig and many others who were there said that Ruth, jockeying with the Cub dugout, had merely waved a hand, the Babe himself left room open for other interpretations. "They were callin' me big belly and balloon-head," he said of the Cubs, "but I think we had 'em madder by givin' them that ol' lump-in-the-throat sign…. That's like callin' a guy yellow…. I took two strikes and after each one I held up my finger and said, 'That's one' and 'That's two.' That's when I waved to the fence!" After he hit the home run, Ruth said, "I just laughed… laughed to myself going around the bases and thinking, 'You lucky bum…lucky, lucky.'"

WATCHING THE SCOREBOARD

In the olden days, before nationwide radio and television coverage of baseball, there was only one way for fans to keep track of their team's away games—even during the World Series. That was through electric (or even mechanical) scoreboards like this one, which was set up by a local newspaper in Chicago to convey results of the 1929 World Series between the Cubs and the Philadelphia Athletics. Crowds would wait patiently for hours as telegraphers painstakingly received and relayed the scores of a game that must have seemed a world away. These Cubs fans didn't have much to cheer about: After losing the first two games at home, the Cubs grabbed a 3–1 win in Philadelphia, but then suffered two heartbreaking defeats to lose the Series, four games to one.

GHOST SHIP

Kids cluster to watch an early portable TV in front of Brooklyn's Ebbets Field during the 1959 World Series between the Dodgers and the Chicago White Sox. But look closely at the old stadium, and you'll see broken windows and other signs of decrepitude. The Dodgers had departed Brooklyn two seasons earlier, and their six-game victory over the "Go Go" Sox in the 1959 Series marked their first as the Los Angeles Dodgers. For these children, absence hadn't made the heart grow fonder; they soon abandoned the game for something more exciting: the 1960 Chevy's high-tech rear engine.

SAFE OR OUT?

The Giants' Carl Hubbell comes into the plate standing up, either avoiding or failing to avoid the tag of the Yankees' Bill Dickey, in Game Four of the 1937 World Series. Hubbell was called safe by the home-plate umpire, Bill Stewart, which brought a storm of protest from the Yankees. The Bombers must have needed something to keep them awake: While the Giants and Hubbell won this game, 7–3, it was their only victory. The Yanks, in the second of their then-unprecedented four consecutive championships, cruised to a five-game Series win.

WHEN SHOE POLISH SAVED THE DAY

The man on the left is the Milwaukee Braves' Vernal "Nippy" Jones, the definition of a utility player. Nippy's role in the 1957 World Series (two at bats, no hits) was almost nonexistent—except for one glorious moment. In the bottom of the tenth inning of Game Four, with the Braves trailing by a run, pinch hitter Jones jumped away from a pitch by the Yankees' Tommy Byrne. Jones claimed that the pitch had hit him on the foot, but umpire Augie Donatelli disagreed—until Jones retrieved the ball and showed Donatelli a shoe-polish mark. Awarded first, Jones left the game for a pinch runner, and watched as the Braves scored three runs to win. Here, Jones and equipment manager Joe Taylor admire the mark that helped win the game.

THEY DIDN'T KNOW WHAT
WAS COMING

Members of the 1932 National League champion Chicago Cubs and their wives celebrate as they head off to face the New York Yankees in the World Series. The Cubs were a feisty team with a collective hair-trigger temper; they had many reasons to loathe the Yankees, not the least of which was that Babe Ruth, Lou Gehrig, and the rest of the Bombers got all the ink. In terms of bench jockeying, the Cubs held their own during the Series, but on the field it was a different story. Babe Ruth slugged two home runs (including his notorious "called shot"), Gehrig hit .529 with three homers and 9 RBI, the Yanks outscored the Cubs 37–19, and the Series came to a merciful close after just four games.

THE LIP SPIES THE PLATE

The St. Louis Cardinals' Leo Durocher scores on a single by Pepper Martin in the sixth game of the great 1934 World Series. Babe Ruth (covering the Series for the newspapers) had picked Durocher as the potential star of the Series...only to see the Lip go hitless in his first fourteen at bats. "What are you trying to do, make a chump out of me?" Ruth asked, and then took Durocher out for dinner and ordered him to eat scallions. "Greatest cure for a batting slump ever invented," said the Babe. Durocher, complaining that he tasted those scallions for days, proceeded to go seven for his next thirteen, helping carry the Cardinals to the championship.

DOMINANCE, PART ONE

The Yankees' Frank Crosetti tags out the Cincinnati Reds' Bill Werber in Game Two of the 1939 Series. Werber was gunned down by catcher Bill Dickey in a strike-'em-out-throw-'em-out double play, a typical indication of the outmanned nature of the Yankees' competition during their string of four consecutive championships between 1936 and 1939. The Yankees won Game One, 2–1, then shut down the Reds easily in the next three games to seal the sweep, their second in a row. "When a team sweeps you, it's like you weren't even there," moaned Reds' infielder Lonnie Frey. "What a nightmare!"

DOMINANCE, PART TWO

Joe DiMaggio touches them all after blasting a home run in Game Five of the 1949 Series, an easy 10–6 win over the Brooklyn Dodgers that gave the Yankees a World Series championship—their first under new manager Casey Stengel. But Stengel and his Bombers were just getting warmed up. They would go on to win in 1950, 1951, 1952, and 1953, before finally giving someone else a chance in 1954. Being a fan of any other team in the early 1950s must have been intensely frustrating.

HITLESS WONDERS

Though no one could have predicted it, the Chicago White Sox—the famed "Hitless Wonders," who had slugged only seven home runs all season—were about to take control of the 1906 World Series. It was the sixth inning of a scoreless Game Three in a Series that was knotted one to one. Jack Pfiester was pitching for the Cubs, and the bases were loaded with Sox. Frank Isbell was at the plate, and Pfiester struck him out as the picture was taken. But the next batter was a little-known utility infielder named George Rohe, who promptly tripled, breaking open the game. The Sox won, 3–0, and after dropping Game Four, pounded the Cubs' pitching in the last two games to capture their unlikely championship.

A CELEBRATION FOR THE CRAB

Johnny Evers (fourth from left) used to say that he couldn't wear a watch because the electricity in his body would quickly break any watch he strapped onto his wrist. Maybe that was true, maybe not. But no one doubted that "the Crab"—second baseman for the Cubs during their great run in the early 1900s—was a tiny supernova, a brilliant baseball mind hidden behind a sharp tongue, a quick temper, and a love of fighting that encompassed opponents, umpires, and teammates alike. "He'd make you want to punch him," said one-time teammate Rabbit Maranville, "but you knew Johnny was thinking only of the team."

THE ROYAL ROOTERS

Boston Brave Hank Gowdy (in baseball uniform, center) poses with a posse of his home city's notorious Royal Rooters, led by Boston mayor John Francis "Honey Fitz" Fitzgerald (third from left) in 1914. Angry at being shut out of the final game at Fenway Park during the 1912 Series, the Rooters had staged an on-field demonstration that had required mounted police to dispel. Two years later, when the perennial doormat "Miracle Braves" won thirty-four of their last forty-four games to take the N.L. pennant, the team made sure to welcome Honey Fitz and his Rooters. The fan support must have helped, as the Braves went on to shock the defending champion Philadelphia Athletics in a four-game sweep.

A LIFELONG LOVE AFFAIR BEGINS

Fans young and old gather outside Brooklyn's Ebbets Field to await the start of a 1920 World Series game between their beloved Robins (soon to be more widely known as the Dodgers) and the Cleveland Indians. From the start, Brooklynites adored their rough-and-tumble, blue-collar team, which seemed to reflect the spirit of its home borough. Two decades later, when the Dodgers began the magnificent run that took them to seven World Series between 1941 and 1956, many of these same young fans, all grown up, were undoubtedly there to cheer on the team again. By the way, Brooklyn lost the 1920 Series to the Indians. That, too, was good preparation for the future.

KISS OF VICTORY

As cheering Cleveland fans look on, future Hall of Famer Tris Speaker receives a big smooch from his mom to celebrate the successful end of the 1920 World Series. Player-manager Speaker, star of two earlier Series with the Boston Red Sox, batted .320 in the 1920 contest against the Brooklyn Robins, but it was Stan Coveleski's three dominating wins (he gave up a total of two runs in twenty-seven innings) that carried the Indians to victory over the Robins. Somewhere off-camera, his mom was probably kissing him, too.

"AND THAT'S THE FOUL LINE...."

Umpires discuss the ground rules with New York Giants player-coach Dave Bancroft (second from left) and New York Yankees player-coach Roger Peckinpaugh (far right) prior to the start of the first game of the 1921 World Series at the Polo Grounds. It's hard to imagine what they were talking about: Peckinpaugh and Bancroft were smart veterans, and their managers—the Yanks' Miller Huggins and the Giants' John McGraw—possessed two of the most brilliant baseball minds of all time. What's more, the Yankees played all of their home games at the Polo Grounds, the Giants' home field, in 1921. There was nothing about this ballpark that both teams didn't know.

DRESS FOR SUCCESS

Socks, underwear, garters: How many of the fans who flocked to the Polo Grounds to watch the all-New York 1921 Series between the Giants and the Yankees had visited the stores advertised on the park's outfield walls? From the look of the crowd, most had spent their money on dark suits, white shirts, and gray hats. Regardless, the well-dressed fans saw an excellent best-of-nine Series, featuring Babe Ruth's first October appearance with the Yankees (he hit just one homer), brilliant pitching by the Yankees' Waite Hoyt and the Giants' Jesse Barnes, and three consecutive tense victories by the Giants to win, five games to three.

RUTH'S FRUSTRATION

It's almost forgotten now, but Babe Ruth had a difficult introduction to World Series baseball after joining the Yankees. In the 1921 Series, his first with the team, he hit just four singles and a lone home run (in a losing cause) while battling injuries that limited him to just six of the eight games. Ruth's struggles must have provided grim entertainment to Giants manager John McGraw, who loathed the attention-getting young slugger. "Why shouldn't we pitch to Babe Ruth?" he asked on the eve of this Series. "We pitch to better hitters in the National League." In 1921, at least, he wasn't punished for his hubris.

THEY WERE GIANTS

Hard to imagine today, but Babe Ruth's Yankees were decided under-dogs when they took on John McGraw's Giants in 1921. Though Yankees fans took some hope as their team jumped out to a 2–0 lead in the Series, reality returned as the Giants won five of the next six games to win the championship, 5–3. Here, the Giants' Jesse Barnes scores on Dave Bancroft's single in Game Six. Barnes was the star of the Series, pitching an astonishing 16 $\frac{1}{3}$ innings in relief, bailing out an ineffective Fred Toney twice to win, and—as if that weren't enough—collecting four hits in nine at bats.

ONSLAUGHT

The Giants' Dave Bancroft and Heinie Groh score on Irish Meusel's single to tie Game One of the 1922 Series, 2–2, in the eighth inning. Frank Frisch, sliding into third, scored a few moments later to give the Giants a 3–2 win and first blood in the Series. For the Yankees, 1922 was more of the same, only worse. While they'd at least competed hard in losing the 1921 Series, they were completely outmatched by the Giants in 1922, hitting just .203 as a team, compared to the Giants' .309. Could it be that the Yankees were good enough to capture the A.L. pennant, but not to win the World Series?

BABE RUTH, SERIES CHOKER?

That's what fans were wondering when the Yankees faced the Giants for the second consecutive Series in 1922. The Babe was coming off a miserable regular season by his standards (.315 with just thirty-five home runs), and the Series was a nightmare for him. "Throw a slow curve at his goddamned feet," manager John McGraw responded when asked how to pitch to the Babe—and the strategy worked. This daring slide under Heinie Groh's tag was just about Ruth's only highlight, as he batted .118 and the Giants manhandled the hapless Yankees, who failed to win a single game.

Groh   Huggins   Ruth.

Worlds Series 1922.

STARSTRUCK

A stellar assortment gathers for the 1924 World Series between the New York Giants and Washington Senators. From left to right, Fred Lieb (writer and official scorer), Nick Altrock (baseball clown), Ty Cobb (prickly superstar), Babe Ruth (legend), John McGraw (Giants manager), Walter Johnson (the Senators' brilliant pitcher), George Sisler (Hall of Fame hitter), and Christy Walsh (Ruth's business manager and ghostwriter). Wonder if Ruth and McGraw—bitter combatants in the past three World Series—had anything to say to each other?

MOB SCENE

Washington Senators fans, hungry for a championship, mass on the field at Griffith Park prior to a 1924 Series game. Their eagerness was rewarded, as the Senators defeated the Giants in seven games, riding on the strong shoulders of their perennial ace, thirty-six-year-old Walter Johnson. After the final game, wrote Fred Lieb, "Congressmen, department heads, merchants, barbers, bootblacks, janitors, office secretaries—all joined in the frivolity. They blew trumpets and beat drums—some beat washbasins with large spoons. Anything that could make a noise was being used in this joyous paean to victory."

GATHERING OF GREATS

A Hall of Fame–filled action shot from the magnificent 1924 Series: The Washington Senators' Goose Goslin is nipped at first on a grounder. New York Giants first baseman Bill Terry has just fielded the throw from shortstop Travis Jackson, seen in the background to the left of Goslin. Second baseman Frank Frisch (background, right), another Hall of Famer, looks on. After the Series was over, with Walter Johnson and the underdog Senators having prevailed, baseball commissioner Kenesaw Mountain Landis wondered, "Are we looking at the zenith of baseball?"

OUT!

An exciting moment from 1926, a classic World Series in a decade full of them: The Yankees' Bob Meusel is thrown out at the plate in Game Five by the St. Louis Cardinals' right fielder, Billy Southworth, with catcher Bob O'Farrell applying the tag. The Yanks won this game anyway, 3–2 in ten innings, but the Cards had the last laugh. In Game Seven, in what may be the single most famous World Series moment of all time, old Grover Cleveland Alexander came in to strike out Tony Lazzeri with the bases loaded to preserve the Cardinals' lead. Two innings later, St. Louis had its first-ever championship.

HIGH TECHNOLOGY

A scattering of fans—most likely natives of New York or St. Louis—cluster around a small chalk scoreboard set up at a railroad station in Los Angeles to get the results of a 1926 World Series game between the Yankees and the Cardinals. A telegrapher at the ballpark would tap out the play-by-play. If the lines were working, and the man in Los Angeles was paying attention, then fans far from the ballpark could get at least a flavor of what they were missing. In many cities, such scoreboards would draw large crowds, but in 1926 the West Coast had its own Pacific Coast League filled with stars, and the majors must have seemed to be located on some distant planet.

QUICK! SEE IF HIS FINGERS WERE WET!

Lew Burdette flashes an A-OK after shutting out the powerful Yankees, 5–0, in Game Seven of the 1957 World Series, giving his Milwaukee Braves their first-ever championship. It was Burdette's third victory in the Series and second straight shutout. Though he admitted it only after his career was over, it was common knowledge that Burdette's out pitch was the illegal spitball—"the best spitter in baseball," according to the Yankees' Whitey Ford. How common was the knowledge? Writing in the *New York Times* the day after the Series ended, columnist Red Smith called Burdette "Chief Slobber on Stitches."

THE SLUGGER

Frank "Home Run" Baker of the Philadelphia Athletics in action. Today, Baker's nickname seems little more than the answer to a trivia question ("Who was called 'Home Run' because he hit two round-trippers in a World Series?"), but the truth was that by the standards of the dead-ball era, Baker was a great slugger. In 1912, when he led the A.L. with ten homers, only three A.L. teams (including the Athletics) hit more than twenty during the entire season. Despite numbers that now seem laughably low, Baker was, in his time, as feared a hitter as any in baseball history, fully worthy of his enshrinement in the Hall of Fame... and his nickname.

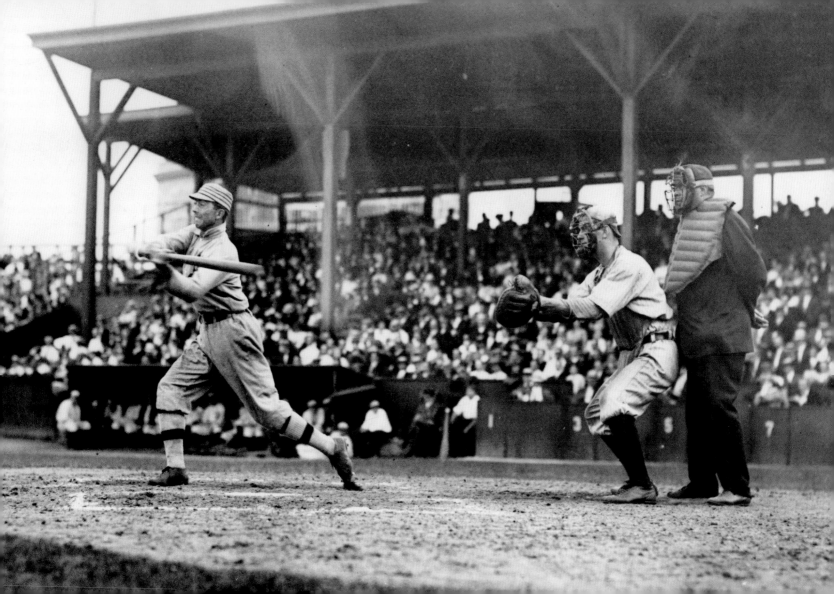

THE CZAR

Firm, stoical, often humorless, Judge Kenesaw Mountain Landis was also unimpeachably honest—making him exactly what baseball needed in its first commissioner as the game reeled in the wake of the shocking Black Sox scandal of 1919. In October 1920, soon after the scandal broke, *The Sporting News* attempted to reassure disgusted fans: "There are still scandal spots to be reached that so far have not been touched, but they will be, and when the work that is to be done has been accomplished we can feel pretty well assured that not in this day and generation will we again have the game smeared with the slime of the crooks who are now being unearthed."

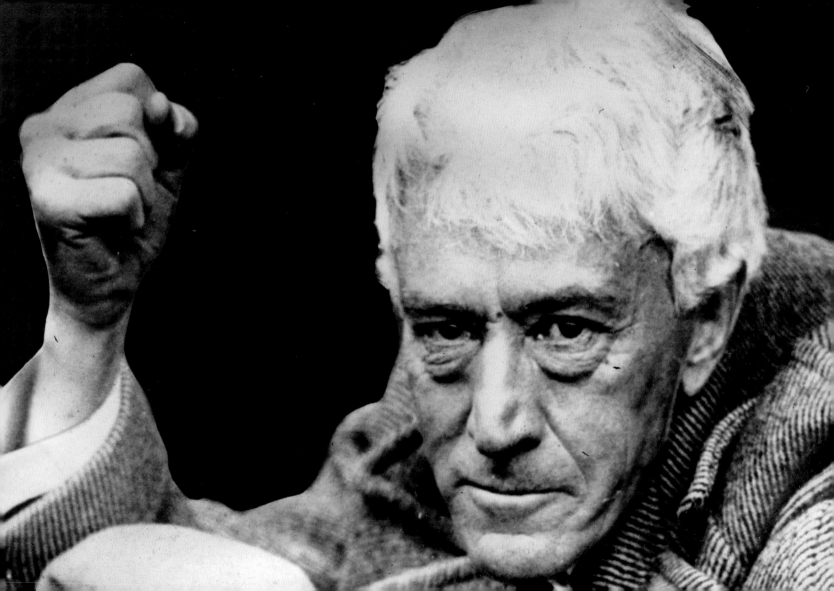

ALL SMILES

Joe Jackson (standing, second from right), Chick Gandil (middle row, second from right), and Eddie Cicotte (front row, third from left) seem happy and relaxed after clinching the American League pennant in 1919. But dark forces may already have been at work in the form of gamblers paying these and other Sox to throw the upcoming World Series. Rumors of skullduggery abounded during the Series, and soon after a suspiciously easy championship went to the Cincinnati Reds, White Sox owner Charles Comiskey offered a $10,000 reward to any-one producing evidence that it had been fixed. A year later the truth began to emerge, though no one ever collected Comiskey's reward.

BAD PENNY

If ever a player put a blight on baseball during a long career, it was Hal Chase. Wherever he went—and he played for five teams between 1905 and 1919—rumors of crooked play and thrown ballgames followed him. And yet, despite efforts by Highlanders manager George Stallings, Reds manager Christy Mathewson, and others to banish him, nothing was done until 1919, just before the Black Sox scandal, in which he apparently played a role. The damage to baseball was incalculable, as Fred Lieb pointed out in *Baseball As I Have Known It*. "How many good young ballplayers may have said, 'Chase gets by with it, year after year, so why shouldn't we pick up a little extra money when the chance is offered us?'" Lieb wrote. "And how many, when tempted, fell?"

INCORRIGIBLE

New York Highlanders first baseman Hal Chase tags out teammate Jeff Sweeney in a rare spring-training action shot taken in Gray, Georgia, in 1909. As early as this, the twenty-six-year-old Chase (acknowledged as his generation's preeminent glove man at his position) was apparently already heading down a crooked path. The man with the "corkscrew brain," as one contemporary observer put it, had a variety of methods to influence the score. One favorite trick was "to arrive at first base for a throw from another infielder just a split second too late," wrote Fred Lieb.

CHASE TRIUMPHANT

Amazingly, despite rampant rumors of his crooked play, in 1910 Hal Chase succeeded in having popular and successful Highlanders manager George Stallings fired and himself named the new manager. ("God, what a way to run a ballclub!" declared Highlanders teammate Jimmy Austin to writer Lawrence Ritter fifty years later, still shaking his head over the mess.) This photograph shows the celebration attending his ascension to manager, but in truth it was a wake. Chase drove the Highlanders into the ground (on purpose?) before resigning after one year, only to throw games for four other teams before his way-too-late expulsion from baseball in 1919.

TWO MEN OUT

Lefty Williams and Eddie Cicotte, two Chicago White Sox pitchers with superb stuff and no moral compass. Williams may have taken to the job of throwing the 1919 World Series with more gusto than anyone, going 0–3 with an atrocious 6.61 ERA and giving up four runs while getting only one out in the first inning of the Series-ending eighth game. With 208 career wins before his expulsion, Cicotte would have had a good shot at getting into the Hall of Fame if he'd stayed away from the gamblers.

SHINE-BALL KING

Before 1920, a variety of trick pitches, including the spitball, emery ball, and other pitches using scuffed-up baseballs were either legal or winked at by the authorities. Eddie Cicotte's contribution to the genre was a superb shine ball, created by darkening and scuffing one side of the ball with dirt and slicking up the white side with sweat or paraffin. Not only did the ball break in unpredictable ways, it spun like a satellite in the night sky, showing its white, reflective side only in flashes. Batters had the devil's own time seeing it, much less hitting it, and Cicotte built a brilliant career—until the 1919 World Series.

THE ONE WHO KNEW

By far the saddest story of the Black Sox scandal belonged to George "Buck" Weaver, the talented infielder who played superbly—and to win—during the 1919 World Series. But Weaver (left) was banned along with Joe Jackson, Eddie Cicotte, and the others because he knew the fix was in but did not report it. When new baseball czar Judge Landis reaffirmed his expulsion of the eight players, he was very specific. "No player who throws a ballgame, no player that undertakes or promises to throw a ballgame, no player that sits in conference with a bunch of crooked players and gamblers, where the ways and means of throwing a game are discussed and does not promptly tell his club about it, will ever play professional baseball!" the Judge proclaimed.

ONE LONELY MAN

Buck Weaver in happier times. For decades after his banishment from the game, he was still trying to get himself reinstated, but to no avail. In a 1953 letter addressed to "Mr. Commission" (Commissioner Ford Frick), he was still trying: "I was suspended for doing some thing wrong which I knew nothing about. I played the 1919 World Series and played a perfect Series. I also hit around .340 [Actually, .324]. I stood trial and was acquitted. You know Commission the only thing we have left in this world is our Judge and the 12 jurors and they found me not guilty. They do some funny things in base ball." But there was nothing funny in the life of Buck Weaver.

THE SUPERSTAR

Joe Jackson had already written his ticket to Cooperstown when he got caught up in the Black Sox scandal. A lifetime .356 hitter when he was banned at age thirty-one, he would likely have reached 3,000 career hits if he'd stayed in the game. Over the years since the scandal broke, much has been made of the fact that Jackson hit .375 for the Series. But, as the 1920 *Reach Guide* put it succinctly: "Jackson testified that he got $5,000 for throwing the games…. Jackson also said that throughout the series he either struck out or else hit easy balls when hits would have meant runs." Imagine what he would have hit if he'd really been trying.

THREE AT THE PEAK

Three of the greatest ballplayers ever to play the game (left to right): Joe Jackson, Ty Cobb, and Napoleon Lajoie. Cobb (.367 lifetime batting average, 4,191 hits) went into the Hall of Fame in 1936, in the first class ever elected. Lajoie (.338, 3,242) followed in 1937. Jackson (.356 average through 1920), on the other hand, was reduced to playing semipro ball and, later, working in small shops while trying to clear his name. Now that nearly all who saw him play are dead, Jackson's pigeon-toed stance at the plate and the graceful yet powerful way he would whip his bat, Black Betsy, through the strike zone are virtually forgotten. All that remains is the memory of a man who threw it all away.

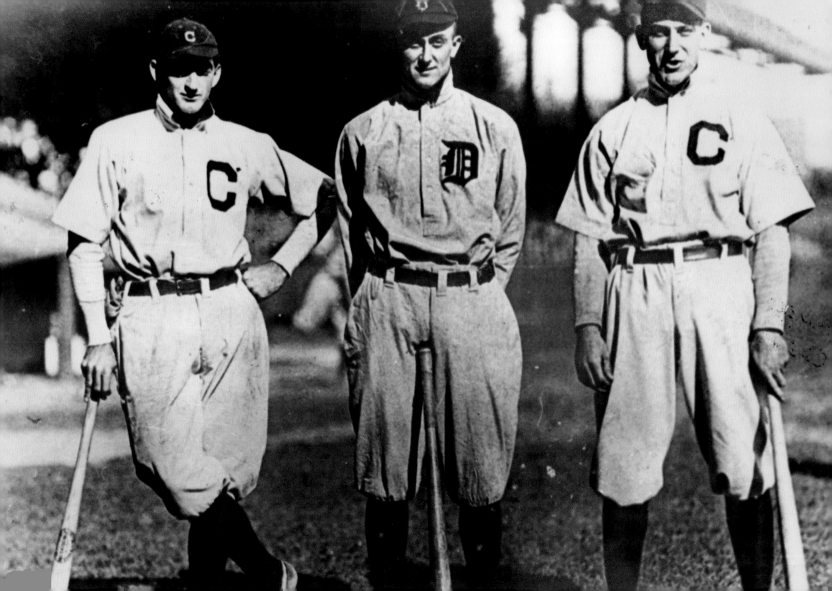

THE RAVAGES OF TIME

Fearfully aged, forty-three-year-old Joe Jackson struggles to make ends meet playing semipro ball in 1932. Jackson, Buck Weaver, and the other banned players lurked like lost spirits around the periphery of major-league baseball for years after the game turned its back on them. In *My Baseball Diary*, James T. Farrell recalls an attempted barnstorming tour in 1922 involving Jackson and other Black Sox. The tour began in Chicago, once the site of the players' greatest triumph. "They played at a small park in Grand Crossing, at Seventy-fifth Street and the Illinois Central tracks," Farrell wrote. "A crowd of about 2,000 saw this game. Joe Jackson hit one ball over the railroad tracks. The barnstorming trip was a failure."

TARNISHED GLORY

Hod Eller was a fine pitcher for the 1920 N.L. champion Cincinnati Reds, going 19–9 with a 2.39 ERA. His specialty, like Eddie Cicotte's, was the "shine ball," the scuffed-up, dirty ball that darted erratically across the plate. Unlike Cicotte, though, Eller pitched to win in the 1919 World Series, winning two games (including the eighth and final one) and becoming perhaps the Reds' premier hero of the Series. But once the scandal broke, his Series achievements immediately became suspect. Had he prevailed only because the Sox intended to lose? Further, after major-league baseball cracked down on freak pitches like the shine ball, Eller's career came to a sudden end when he was only twenty-six.

THE RINGLEADER

If not for the Black Sox scandal, Chick Gandil would be remembered today as a useful journeyman ballplayer during the dead-ball era. Instead, his name will long represent greed and stupidity. Gandil, like most other members of the White Sox, was woefully underpaid by owner Charles Comiskey ("a sarcastic, belittling man who was the tightest owner in baseball," Gandil said). It's not surprising, therefore, that the thirty-two-year-old Gandil, his career waning, might offer to enlist teammates to fix the 1919 Series. Or that he would first approach Cicotte, who was thirty-five and shared the same concerns. The two then brought the other players aboard, receiving $10,000 for their pains.

GANDIL'S TALE

You could dress him up, but you couldn't disguise those eyes: Chick Gandil looks for the main chance, as always, a few years after his baseball career ended. In a remarkable interview published in *Sports Illustrated* in 1956, the sixty-eight-year-old Gandil said, "To this day I feel that we got what we had coming." When asked why he and Eddie Cicotte—the first two in on the scheme—chose to approach Joe Jackson, Buck Weaver, Happy Felsch, Swede Risberg, Joe McMullin, and Lefty Williams, Gandil said it wasn't "that we loved them, because there never was much love among the White Sox. Let's just say that we disliked them the least."

IT'S GREAT TO BE A YANKEE, PART ONE

Elston Howard, Whitey Ford, Tony Kubek, and Sal Maglie assume a familiar position for a Yankee player in September in the 1950s: winning a game and then waiting around to hear if you've clinched the pennant yet. In this case, in 1957, Casey Stengel's stars had to wait another day before clinching, but the outcome was never in doubt, as the team went 98–56 and won the A.L. by eight games. The World Series was a shock, though, as the Bombers fell to Lew Burdette, Hank Aaron, and the Milwaukee Braves in seven. It was the Yankees' second Series defeat in three years—and an early sign that the team could no longer walk on the field in October and expect to win.

IT'S GREAT TO BE A YANKEE, PART TWO

It was teamwork all the way as starter Spec Shea (left) pitched five innings, ace reliever Joe Page (right) pitched four, and Yogi Berra caught all nine as the Yankees defeated Ralph Branca and the Dodgers, 5–3, in Game One of the 1947 World Series. Shea started three games (winning two) and Page relieved four times (and pitched five shutout innings in the Bombers' Game Seven clincher) as the Yankees broke the Dodgers' hearts...and not for the last time.

AND SOMETIMES IT'S EVEN GREAT TO BE A DODGER

Don Bessent drenches Pee Wee Reese with beer as a happy Carl Erskine looks on. The three Dodgers were celebrating the 1956 pennant clincher—the second straight time the team had won the N.L. flag. For the first time, though, they'd be entering the World Series as defending champions, having beaten the hated Yankees in 1955. And how close they came to making it two in a row! After a spectacular one-hit, ten-inning shutout by Clem Labine in Game Six (a feat that would be celebrated today if it hadn't taken place the day after the Yankees' Don Larsen threw his perfect game), the Series was deadlocked at three games apiece. But Game Seven was a nightmare for Don Newcombe and the Dodgers, as the Yanks pounded Newk and rolled to an easy 9–0 victory.

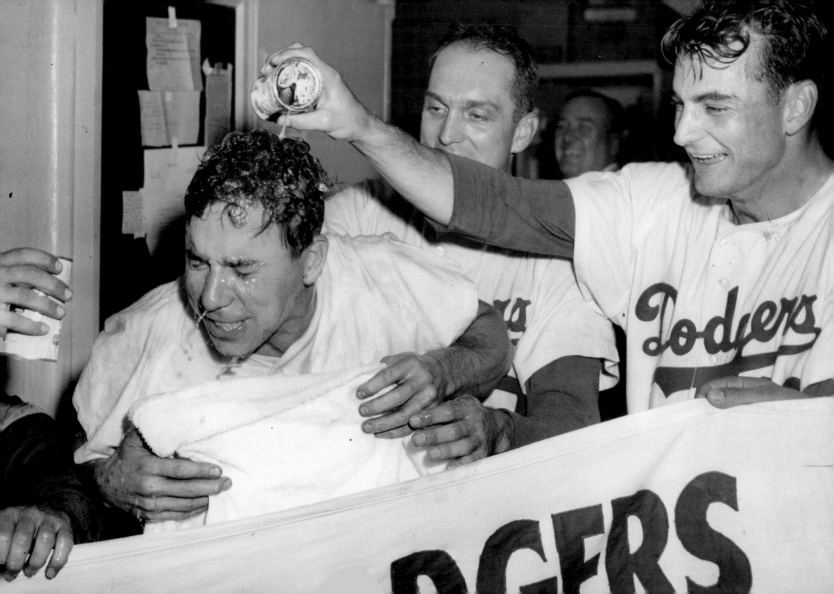

R&R

Neither of them reached six feet or 180 pounds. But Pee Wee Reese (left) and Phil Rizzuto cast a giant shadow across New York—and major-league baseball—throughout the 1940s and well into the 1950s, patrolling shortstop and leading the Dodgers and Yankees to a combined sixteen World Series, including six against each other. For most of their careers, it was Rizzuto who was left grinning, as the Yanks defeated the Bums in 1941, 1947, 1949, 1952, and 1953. In 1955, their last head-to-head confrontation, Reese finally got his chance to smile, as Brooklyn won its only championship.

THEY BOTH LOOKED LIKE PRESIDENTS

Washington Senators great Walter Johnson (right) seems Lincolnesque in front of the White House in this photograph, and President Calvin Coolidge (second from left) doesn't look so bad himself. Team owner Clark Griffith (left) and player-manager Bucky Harris round out the foursome. In 1924 the Senators answered all of Washington's hopes and dreams by capturing the World Series over the New York Giants. The victory gave the thirty-six-year-old Johnson his first Series ring, and even some of the Giants didn't begrudge him. "Walter Johnson is such a lovable guy that the good Lord didn't want to see him beat again," said pitcher Jack Bentley.

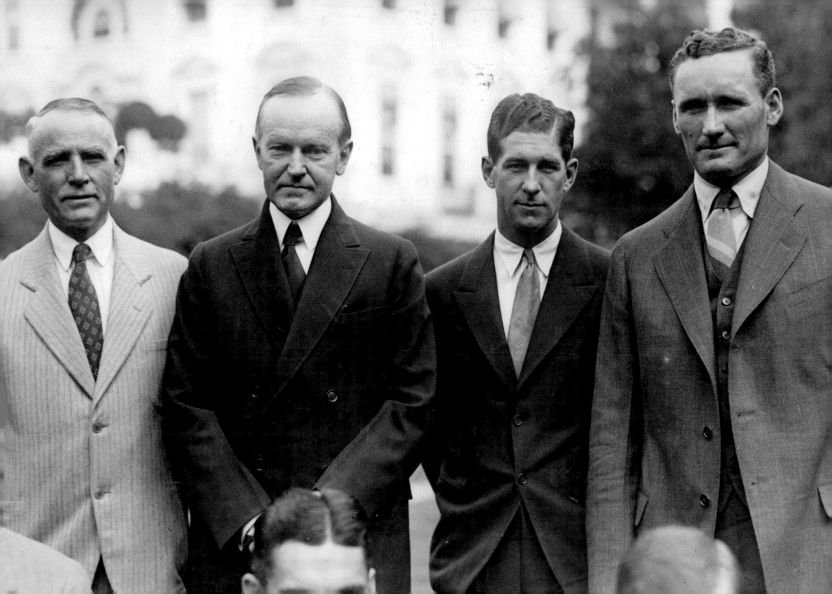

CLASH OF THE TITANS

The Dodgers' Pee Wee Reese heads around second in the sixth inning of the long, messy Game Six of the 1947 Series. (The Dodgers scored four runs in the inning and won the game, 8–6.) The first of a string of six wildly entertaining clashes between the two teams over the next decade, the 1947 contest was a back-and-forth melee featuring perhaps the finest World Series catch of all time, Al Gionfriddo's grab over the bullpen fence of Joe DiMaggio's 415-foot Game Six clout. (Or, as columnist Joe Williams, apparently a Yankees fan, put it: "Some anony-mous character on the Brooklyn team leaped clear out of the park to take a home run from the only real big-league ballplayer in the series.")

THE GAME HAD CHANGED, AT LAST

An important moment in Game Six of the 1947 World Series—Eddie Stanky scoring on Pee Wee Reese's hit to put the Dodgers ahead in the sixth inning—reflects something far more important and long-lasting: evidence that baseball's wall of racial exclusion and intolerance had finally been breached. Approaching the plate from the back is rookie Jackie Robinson, the first African-American ballplayer to reach the major leagues in the twentieth century. Number 23 is Dodgers pitcher Dan Bankhead, the first black pitcher allowed into the game after the color line fell. Others—many others—were on their way, but these two strong, talented men were the first.

ALL FOR ONE

It was a remarkable thing about the relationship between the Brooklyn Dodgers players and their fans: Sometimes it was hard to tell them apart. Q: Can you spot ace Brooklyn reliever Hugh Casey in this joyful photo? It was taken after Casey threw one pitch in Game Four of the 1947 Series, induced a double play, and got the win when Cookie Lavagetto broke up Bill Bevens' no-hit bid with a two-run double in the bottom of the ninth. A: That's Hugh smiling at the camera, center right, clasping the bartender's hand. Bringing player and fans even closer together was the fact that the bar was Casey's own establishment on Flatbush Avenue, a place where Dodgers fans were welcome and Yankees fans—if any ever ventured into Brooklyn—kept quiet.

SQUABBLE

Young Yogi Berra—a twenty-two-year-old rookie in 1947—had a terrible time in the Series that year, batting just .158 and struggling in the field. ("Never in a World Series have I seen such awful ketchin'," said Connie Mack, who'd been around for every Series since the first in 1903.) But Yogi had time to improve: The 1947 classic was the first of an astonishing fourteen World Series for Berra, whose 259 Series at bats, seventy-one hits, ten doubles, twelve home runs, forty-one runs scored, 39 RBI, and thirty-two walks all rank in the top three of all time. "He'd fall in a sewer and come up with a gold watch," said Casey Stengel of the homely catcher who became a multiple MVP and lock Hall of Famer.

"LET'S PLAY TWO!"

Fans flock to Wrigley Field, one of the coziest of all ballparks—and one of the best for hitters, then and now. In the 1930s, when this photo was taken, it was an especially cozy locale for the hometown Cubs, who captured the National League pennant that year. Unfortunately, in the World Series the Detroit Tigers took three out of four games played at Wrigley and won the championship behind the booming bat of recent World War II returnee Hank Greenburg. Still, at the time no could have guessed that the Cubs' 1945 pennant would be their last of the twenti-eth century.

THE CLOWN IS A GENIUS

Casey Stengel seems small, goofy, even unsure of himself when surrounded by baseball men as the 1949 World Series begins. (Left to right,
that's American League president Will Harridge, Commissioner Happy
Chandler, N.L. president Ford Frick, and Dodgers manager Burt Shotton.)
It's barely remembered today, but the selection of Stengel—who had a
long-standing reputation as a clown—was widely considered an act of
lunacy by the usually steadfast Yankees management. "The general
consensus," said Yankees executive Lee MacPhail years later, "was that
Stengel simply didn't fit in with the Yankees, that image of dignity, class,
refinement." Five years and five World Championships later, nobody
minded.

ANOTHER YEAR, ANOTHER CHAMPIONSHIP

Even the crowd of 68,000 seems subdued as they leave Yankee Stadium following Game Four of the 1950 World Series, a 5–2 Whitey Ford win that completed the Bombers' minimalist sweep of the "Whiz Kid" Philadelphia Phillies. (The score of the four games was 1–0, 2–1, 3–2, and 5–2, yet no one ever thought the Phillies, having lost several of their best players to military service or injuries, had a chance.) It was the second of the Yankees' still-record five consecutive Series victories from 1949 through 1953, but the other four—all against either the Brooklyn Dodgers or New York Giants—were a lot more fun.

I'M OLD-FASHIONED

In the early years of the World Series, before the coming of radio and television, mechanical scoreboards were a necessity—a lifeline for baseball fans far from the ballpark. By 1950, when this photo was taken, scoreboards like the one perched here in the second-floor typewriter-shop window at Fulton Street and Broadway in Manhattan were a novelty, but they enabled shoppers and other passersby to grab a moment to catch up on the Yankees-Phillies confrontation. Given that the Series was a sweep for the Bombers, these fans probably liked what they saw.

TWO TOUGH GUYS

They didn't come any feistier than these two, the magnificent pitcher Robert "Lefty" Grove and his Philadelphia Athletics teammate, catcher Mickey Cochrane. "The fire in his arm was matched by the quick blaze of his temper," wrote Robert Smith of Grove, while Tom Meany and Lee Allen said that Cochrane had "the fighting spirit of a Marine battalion." Together, under the leadership of dignified manager Connie Mack, Grove and Cochrane drove the Athletics to three consecutive A.L. pennants (1929–31) and two championships.

HERE'S YOUR RING, WHAT'S YOUR HURRY?

Receiving his 1947 World Series ring from Commissioner Happy Chandler in the spring of 1948, Yankees manager Bucky Harris must have thought he was beginning a long, fulfilling stretch with the team. But the sand was already running through the hourglass for him. In 1948 the defending World Champion Yankees would plummet all the way to third place—though with a 94–60 record—and Harris had personality conflicts with the strong-willed Yankees executives. Shockingly, he was fired after the season, just his second as manager. Even more shockingly, he was replaced by the journeyman player, failed major-league skipper, and all-around clown named Casey Stengel. What on earth were the Yankees thinking?

BUCKY'S PEAK

The 1920s and 1930s were the age of the player-manager, and one of the most famous was Bucky Harris, here sliding safely into third during Game Two of the 1924 World Series. The Washington Senators' second baseman since 1919, he was named manager as well in 1924—and immediately took the Senators to their first-ever American League pennant. Then, with a succession of brilliant managerial moves (using Fred Marberry as one of the first true relief aces in baseball history, bringing an aging and exhausted Walter Johnson in to pitch four innings in Game Seven) and his own superb play, he piloted the team to a classic Series victory.

HANK WAS EVERYWHERE

Hank Gowdy had a long career as a part-time catcher with the Boston Braves and New York Giants. In the seventeen years he spent behind the plate, he had one moment of true on-field glory: the 1914 World Series, when he hit .545 with three doubles, a triple, and a home run in the Miracle Braves' stunning four-game sweep of the mighty Philadelphia Athletics. Today, however, Gowdy's fame rests chiefly on the fact that he was the first major-league player to enlist in World War I, a move that was widely hailed—and endlessly photographed— at the time. Here Hank, in military uniform as usual, collects money for the Athletic Fund at New York's Polo Grounds while attending the 1917 World Series between the Giants and the Chicago White Sox.

THREE IMMORTALS

The World Series has always been a gathering spot for great stars of the past and present. The 1929 Series between the Philadelphia Athletics and the Chicago Cubs was no exception, as this photo of George Sisler, Babe Ruth, and Ty Cobb shows. Sisler was just coming off his last big year (.326 with 205 hits for the Boston Braves), and Cobb was a season into his retirement after twenty-four years in the game. Only the Babe, himself thirty-four, still had a few moments of glory left: seasons of forty-nine and forty-six home runs and one last glorious World Series moment, his classic "called shot" of 1932.

THEY SHOULD HAVE CALLED HIM "BUGS"

He's mostly remembered today as a slick fielder with a funny name, but during his twenty-three-year career with the Boston Braves and other teams, Rabbit Maranville (center, holding the basket) got plenty of headlines. He was smart, funny, noisy, and unpredictable—a combustible combination. In his *New Historical Baseball Abstract*, Bill James lists some of Rabbit's most spectacular escapades—getting arrested in Japan after swiping a military uniform and trying to march in a parade, painting iodine all over an umpire's face during a game in the guise of treating a cut. James concludes by saying, "You and I will never see the likes of him." More's the pity!

THE ACE

Charles Albert "Chief" Bender's lifetime records are very good, but not great: 212 wins, mostly with the Philadelphia Athletics, a career 2.46 ERA compiled largely during the dead-ball era. But at the time he was considered one of the game's giants, up in the stratosphere with Christy Mathewson and Three Finger Brown. Connie Mack, who managed Bender in Philadelphia and saw nearly every pitcher of the first half of the twentieth century, put it best: "If I had all the men I've ever handled and they were in their prime and there was one game I wanted to win above all others, Albert would be my man."

ABOUT TO TOUCH FOUR

The San Francisco Giants' Chuck Hiller descends on home plate after slugging a grand-slam home run to break open Game Four of the 1962 World Series against the Yankees. Matty Alou (#41) greets Hiller at the plate while Yankees catcher Elston Howard looks on disconsolately. This Series, filled with breathless moments, come-from-behind victories, brilliant pitching, and timely hitting, was one of the greatest of all time. It was also the last hurrah of the dynastic Yankees of the 1950s and early 1960s, as they rode an exceptional performance by pitcher Ralph Terry to a 1–0 Game Seven victory. It would be the Bombers' final championship for fifteen years.

A KISS ON "THE LIP"

Giants manager Leo Durocher with his son Chris at the tail end of the exhausting, exhilarating 1951 season. No one since Babe Ruth left a bigger mark on baseball than Durocher, eternally arguing with umpires, getting suspended, and generally raising a ruckus. But perhaps his most brazen act was switching from managing the Brooklyn Dodgers to the New York Giants midway through the 1948 season, a move that was met with deep suspicion by Giants fans. Durocher's reaction? "I stiffened my neck and vowed that, like me or not, I was going to give them a ballclub so exciting to watch that they'd come out in spite of me and in spite of themselves." Which is exactly what he did.

HEADSTRONG

A Pittsburgh Pirates fan waits for a game to begin at Yankee Stadium in October 1960. Fortunately for him, the Pirates, after being outscored 46–17 while somehow splitting the first six games of the World Series, brought some big bats of their own to Game Seven. Despite blowing a 4–0 lead, the Pirates entered the bottom of the ninth with the game tied, 9–9. That set the stage for Bill Mazeroski's heroic Series-winning home-run shot, perhaps the single most famous homer in World Series history.

IMAGINE WHAT HE'D SEEN!

Fans wait outside the Polo Grounds for tickets to the 1954 World Series between the Giants and the Cleveland Indians—but these are not just any fans. First in line is Charles M. Kierst (left), a firefighter from Auburn, New York. Kierst had also been first in line for the 1921 Series between the Giants and the Yankees and had attended twenty-eight Series since then. That meant he'd been lucky enough to see Babe Ruth, Lou Gehrig, Joe DiMaggio, and Willie Mays in their glory; John McGraw, Leo Durocher, and Casey Stengel sneering at the opposition; and Walter Johnson, Carl Hubbell, and Dizzy Dean throwing strikes. In other words: virtually the entire history of baseball.

DON'T CROSS THE ROOTERS

Boston's famed "Royal Rooters" march around the field at Fenway Park prior to Game Five of the magnificent 1912 Series between the Red Sox and the New York Giants. Later, when the Series went to eight games (there'd been a tie), the Rooters naturally expected to occupy their usual seats, and were outraged to find that they had been sold to others. The Rooters expressed their displeasure with a noisy demonstration outside that held the crowd down to a paltry 17,000 fans. Those who did attend saw one of the greatest World Series games of all time: the magnificent pitching duel between Christy Mathewson and two Boston pitchers that culminated in the Sox' come-from-behind 3–2 victory.

THE TEEMING MULTITUDES

Fans celebrate in downtown Brooklyn after their Dodgers clinch the 1949 N.L. pennant. "That was the Dodger fan of blessed memory," wrote Leo Durocher in *Nice Guys Finish Last*. "They came to root, and they never gave up. It was Brooklyn against the world. They were not only complete fanatics, but they knew baseball like the fans of no other city…. You don't have fans like that any more. There will never be such fans again. Something went out of baseball when the Dodgers left Brooklyn, and not all the king's horses and all the king's men can ever put it back."

BROADWAY CAVALCADE

Orderly fans look to the heavens in Manhattan's Times Square, in an undated photograph likely taken during one of the three titanic World Series clashes between John McGraw's Giants and Babe Ruth's Yankees between 1921 and 1923. The fans are actually gazing at a mechanical scoreboard, presumably set up just below the enterprising photographer's perch. Not everyone who wanted to could get into the Polo Grounds or (in 1923) the new Yankee Stadium; for these fans, watching the results appear on the scoreboard had to suffice. Broadway shows—and a movie starring popular Norma Talmadge—must have taken quite a beating at the box office that day.

PART OF THE TEAM

Fans stroll out of New York's Polo Grounds, most likely after a World Series game from the 1920s. Stadiums built since the 1980s have tried to duplicate the mood of the old-time ballparks, but even so it's hard to imagine today how close fans felt to their teams during the early decades of baseball. The ballparks were almost always located smack in the middle of residential neighborhoods: You'd get off the bus, the subway, or the trolley and walk up to the ticket booth. Players worked "regular" jobs in the off-season, often side by side with the same men and women who would be sitting in the bleachers cheering them on from April into October. Those days will never come again.

THE OUTSIDERS

Between them, slugging outfielders Ralph Kiner (left) and Hank Sauer played twenty-five seasons of major-league ball. They hit a combined 657 home runs, drove in 1,891 runs, and were selected to eight All-Star teams. What else did they have in common? Neither of them ever got a sniff of World Series play. It takes luck as well as skill to make it to the big stage.

COKE AND A SMILE

Brooklyn Dodgers (standing, left to right) Hugh Casey, Pee Wee Reese, Joe Hatten, and Ed Stanky form a happy chain with a seated Dixie Walker after the Dodgers' 9–8 victory in Game Three of the memorable 1947 Series. After falling behind two games to none, the Dodgers fought their way back, all the way to Game Seven...which the Yankees won, as they always seemed to in those days. You couldn't blame Hugh Casey for the unhappy ending: The reliever pitched in six of the seven games, and brilliantly, giving up just five hits and a single run in 10 ⅓ innings, winning two games and saving another. But it wasn't enough.

HEART OF NEW YORK CITY

How important were the New York baseball teams to the city during the first half of the twentieth century? They received a hero's welcome from thousands of fans just for winning the pennant! Here, serenaded by a brass band, the New York Giants march up the steps of City Hall between teams representing the police and fire departments after capturing the 1933 flag. The enthusiasm was understandable: It was the Giants' first pennant in nine years—and their first without longtime manager John McGraw, who'd retired during the 1932 season.

THE MVPS

"You gotta have a catcher or you'll have a lot of passed balls," said Casey Stengel. And Ol' Case had one of the best of all time: the Yankees' Yogi Berra, shown here behind the plate. Yogi was the dominant A.L. catcher during the 1950s, hitting twenty-plus homers ten years running, winning three Most Valuable Player awards, and helping lead the Yankees to a stunning fourteen World Series during his nineteen-year career. His counterpart in the N.L. was the Dodgers' Roy Campanella (at bat), who hit 332 home runs and also captured three MVPs during his career. The two magnificent catchers faced each other five times in the World Series. Four (including 1953, pictured here) went to Berra and the Yanks.

DRESSED FOR THE OCCASION

At the turn of the twentieth century, many observers believed that major-league baseball (at the time, just the National League) was doomed by the blight of "rowdyism." Violence at the ballpark seemed uncontrollable: Players fought each other, fans hurled vile epithets and battled in the stands, and everyone ganged up on the umpires. The American League arrived in 1901 with the promise of a clean game, one that women and children could attend—and soon found itself out-stripping the established N.L. in popularity. By the 1920s, when this photograph was taken, a crowd at the Polo Grounds might be as nattily attired as attendees at a fancy dinner party.

THE GANG

Dizzy Dean (far left) and Pepper Martin (far right) bracket other members of the famed St. Louis Cardinals Gashouse Gang. In later years, Leo Durocher (second from left) built a sort of second career telling stories about the gang, mostly about how the Cardinals players—especially Dean—almost drove manager Frank Frisch (third from right) insane with wild pranks. "Those stories are awfully funny when Durocher tells them," Frisch allowed, "but, then, he was only playing with Diz—he didn't have to manage him."

LONG-GONE GREATS

No one wrote more colorfully, or more emotionally, about baseball than sportswriter Grantland Rice (1880–1954). He was referring to sports heroes in general when he penned the following poem, but he could have been describing the 1909 Pittsburgh Pirates, who went 110–42 and won the World Series—but who are virtually forgotten today:

Far off I hear the rolling, roaring cheers
They come to me from many yesterdays,
From record deeds that cross the fading years,
And light the landscape with their brilliant plays,
Great stars that knew their days in fame's bright sun,
I hear tramping to oblivion.

Pennant Winners

PITTSBURG · B·B· CLUB ·
NATIONAL LEAGUE
1909

PITTSBURG

THE BIG BAT

Four stars of the St. Louis Cardinals' 1944 pennant winners (left to right): Whitey Kurowski, Marty Marion, Stan Musial, and Ray Sanders. The first three were great players, but Sanders—a 4-F first baseman whose short career ended soon after the stars returned from World War II—was the unsung hero of the Cards' World Series championship over the St. Louis Browns. Sanders hit .286 and got on base eleven times during the six-game Series, slugging a home run, scoring a team-high five runs, and joining Jimmy Ripple, Al Weis, Brian Doyle, and other journeymen who shone on the biggest stage of all.

INCOGNITO

Yes, that's Babe Ruth in the back row…wearing a New York Giants uniform! Here's the story: After the 1920 season, his first with the Yankees, the Babe joined some of the Giants on a postseason tour of Cuba. Despite leaving his own uniform at home, Ruth had a fine time, making $40,000 in appearance fees, but he lost so much of it betting on the horses in Havana that he had to rely on his wife (who had foresightedly squirreled away some cash) for boat fare home.

LIFE IN A FISHBOWL

Babe Ruth craved attention, but life must have been difficult for his wife, Claire, and daughters, Dorothy and Julia. Here the Babe poses with Dorothy and Claire, flanked by the New York City sporting press. Among the sportswriters clustered in this shot—which dates from the early 1930s—are Ken Smith of the *Graphic*, Tim Cohane and Tom Meany of the *World Telegram* (fourth, fifth, and sixth from left), and Rud Rennie of the *Herald Tribune* (third from right). These were the men who painted the outsize portrait of the Babe the public knew and loved.

COOPERSTOWN ROUND UP

Player-manager Leo Durocher leads his Brooklyn Dodgers charges onto Doubleday Field for the annual Hall of Fame game in 1943—a concession to wartime gasoline restrictions that brought fans to the ballpark via horse, bicycle, and foot. During the season, the flamboyant Leo was almost ridden out of town by stoical Dodgers president Branch Rickey, no fan of his tough-guy style. At season's end, Rickey gave Durocher his unconditional release as a player-manager, saying that he wanted Leo to be free to "sign a contract as a movie actor," a direct shot at Durocher's fondness for Hollywood glitz. But in the end, Durocher returned to manage the team again in 1944.

"NOW PLAYING THIRD BASE... TRIGGER"

In a wartime publicity stunt that delighted Cooperstown fans, the Brooklyn Dodgers rode—instead of throwing around—the old horse-hide while preparing for the 1943 Hall of Fame game. Unfortunately, the Dodgers didn't have enough horses in the pennant race, finishing just 81–72, twenty-three games behind the pennant-winning St. Louis Cardinals. It would be 1947 before the team would make it back to the top of the National League again.

EN ROUTE

Running hard, the Yanks' Phil Rizzuto beats the throw to first during the 1947 Hall of Fame game at Cooperstown's Doubleday Field. In 1947 Rizzuto was twenty-nine and still struggling to regain the skills he'd lost during three World War II seasons. Other young stars never made it back, but Rizzuto would be a part of seven Yankees World Series appearances and six World Championships. Rizzuto made another memorable trip to Cooperstown in 1994, when, after many disappointments, he was finally elected to the Hall of Fame.

IF LOOKS COULD KILL

Robert "Lefty" Grove is dressed to the nines in this undated photograph, but the true spirit of the man comes through in the expression in his gimlet eyes. Grove was as cold-blooded as they came on the mound, claiming more than his share of the plate with his terrifying fastball and devastating curve. He wasn't the All-American Boy, like Christy Mathewson; a statesman, like Walter Johnson; or a canny show-off, like Dizzy Dean. (In the words of historian Ira Smith, Grove was "tops as a 'lobby sitter,' spending hours on end just puffing on long cigars.") But what Lefty did was win, 300 times with the Philadelphia Athletics and the Boston Red Sox.

THAT PITCHER'S THROWING GAS

In this goofy pic, taken in late 1929, Chicago Cubs star Gabby Hartnett watches as Brooklyn Dodgers pitcher Doug McWeeny "fills the tank" of Baby Hartnett's carriage. Back in the days when players held jobs during the off-season, Chicago native McWeeny operated this Windy City gas station. Hartnett would go on to have his best season in 1930 (.339, 37 home runs, 122 RBI), while McWeeny would get traded to the Cincinnati Reds, go 0–2 with a 7.36 ERA, and see his major-league career come to an end. After a season like that, it's a good thing he had a second job to return to.

HE SHOULD HAVE BEEN THERE

"Dave Barnhill [left, with Hall of Famer Buck Leonard] could have been a major league pitching star except for three things: He was too little, too black, and too old. He overcame the first, almost overcame the second, but couldn't lick the third," wrote John Holway in *Black Diamonds.* "When the big league gates were finally opened in 1947, Dave was thirty-three, just too old to go through them." And thus most fans were deprived of the chance to see a pitcher who weighed 125 pounds ("after it had snowed on me," Barnhill said) but threw as hard as Walter Johnson, Lefty Grove, or Sandy Koufax.

THE ALL STARS

The magnificent Negro League All-Star team, posing during their 1945 postseason tour to Venezuela. In the front row, far left, is Jackie Robinson, who had already been signed by Branch Rickey's Dodgers— and who would, of course, break the major league color barrier in 1947. But in 1945 he was just a young man, unsure of his ability to play in the bigs. "Baseball is baseball," roommate Gene Benson (next to Robinson) told him. "Jackie, always remember: Where you're goin' ain't half as tough as where you been."

Top Row

BLANCO CHATAING   ROY CAMPANELLA   MARVIN BARKER   BILL ANDERSON   QUINCY TROUPPE
GEORGE JEFFERSON   PARNELL WOODS   ROY WELMAKER   BUCK LEONARD,   Bottom Row
JACKIE ROBINSON   EUGENE BENSON   FELTON SNOW   VERDEL MATHIS   SAM JETHROE   TRAINER
AMERICAN ALL STARS   MGR.   CARACAS   VENEZUELA

1945

Alegres
Caracas

BASEBALL-MAD IN ANY LANGUAGE

Spreading the game of baseball worldwide has been a mission of the major leagues at least since 1888, when a tour took All-Star teams as far as the great pyramids of Egypt. But no ground was more fertile for the growth of the baseball obsession than Japan. From early in the twentieth century, baseball has been Japan's pastime, as well as America's. Here the San Francisco Giants are greeted in Tokyo as they arrive for a series of postseason games against Japan's strongest teams. The Giants had as much as they could handle during the tour, struggling to score against the Japanese pitchers.

WORTH WAITING FOR!

Wearing their Sunday best and waving a giveaway magazine, young fans amass outside Engel Stadium in Chattanooga, Tennessee, to await the arrival of Walter Johnson. The Big Train, ace pitcher for the Washington Senators for more than two decades, was the rare player who maintained his modesty and unpretentiousness, even as he became a world-famous star, winner of 416 games (second most of all time). "His deeds on the diamond and his fine character combined to make him one of the greatest and most beloved figures in baseball history," wrote Ira Smith.

ELECTIONEERING

The Yankees (including Babe Ruth, second from right, and an amused Lou Gehrig, third from left) come out in force for presidential candidate Al Smith, running against Herbert Hoover in 1928. When Hoover appeared at Yankee Stadium and Ruth was asked to pose with him, the Babe refused, saying "Nothing doing on politics." At other times, though, Ruth made it clear he supported Smith—though not enough to actually vote in the 1928 election, which Hoover won in a landslide.

HIKE!

Babe Ruth (front and center) was a PR man's dream, always willing to pose, no matter how silly he looked. And he always seemed to enjoy what he was doing, as this cheerful photograph demonstrates. Newspaper reporters often described him as a child in a man's body—plain-spoken, unpredictable, prey to temper tantrums, prone to acts of generosity and pettiness alike—and in many ways, they were right. It's typical to see Lou Gehrig in these offbeat photos of Ruth, usually somewhere in the background (here, he's playing tailback), almost always looking amused at his teammate's shenanigans.

HALL OF FAME, HERE I COME

Jackie Robinson starts his swing during the 1951 Hall of Fame game held at Doubleday Field in Cooperstown. The Dodgers had four future Hall of Famers on their club that year: Robinson, Duke Snider, Roy Campanella, and Pee Wee Reese—as well as another star, Gil Hodges, who many believe deserves enshrining as well. In this exhibition game, the Dodgers were playing the Philadelphia Athletics, who came to town with a distinction of their own: They were being managed by Jimmy Dykes, in his first year at the helm. Dykes had just taken over for Connie Mack, who'd managed the team for an astonishing fifty years.

WAIT TILL NEXT YEAR, EMMETT

Dodgers catcher Roy Campanella consoles team mascot Emmett Kelly, world-famous clown, presumably after another galling Dodgers defeat. In 1957, while still based in Brooklyn, the Bums hired Kelly to entertain fans at games at Ebbets Field. (This could be seen as an act of desperation by a team trying to reverse plummeting attendance.) In 1958, newly relocated to Los Angeles, the Dodgers realized that a fresh image was necessary and quickly dumped the sad clown.

PLAY BY PLAY

The St. Louis Cardinals' Leo Durocher (far left) and Joe Medwick (second from right) visit the studio of broadcaster France Laux (standing over CBS microphone) in 1936. Laux was a fixture in St. Louis sports radio for nearly two decades, broadcasting Cardinals games, the World Series, and the All-Star Game, as well as boxing, football, wrestling, hockey, and basketball. He would often be joined in the booth by such talkative "sidekicks" as Durocher, Dizzy Dean, Pepper Martin, and Gabby Street. Laux's self-proclaimed claim to fame: He worked twenty years without ever missing a broadcast or arguing with a player or umpire.

Robertson Fresh
Tampa 10863

"PICK ME! PICK ME!"

Little League aspirants show up for tryouts in Scarsdale, New York, in 1959. In the late 1950s, the league was in its heyday, proclaimed as a force for preventing crime and delinquency, chartered by the United States Congress, and honored with a week of celebration by President Eisenhower. It was also a coast-to-coast phenomenon. The teams that qualified for the playoffs leading to the 1959 Little League World Series included squads from Hamtramck, Michigan; Auburn, California; Gadsden, Alabama; Shippensburg, Pennsylvania; Valleyfield, Quebec; Oahu, Hawaii; and San Juan, Puerto Rico. (By the way, Hamtramck defeated Auburn, 12–0, to win it all.)

BALLPLAYERS ON PARADE

Youth teams parade across Harrison Field, in Newark, New Jersey, in 1915. To the far right an adult player wears the unique uniform of the Baltimore Terrapins, revealing that this photograph was taken before a Federal League game pitting the Terrapins against the hometown Newark Peppers. The Federal League, unveiled in 1914 as a direct challenge to the reigning American and National leagues, lasted only two seasons. But it made plenty of noise while it was there, wooing established stars from the majors with high salaries and giving players a glimpse of freedom they would not taste again until the era of free agency began, sixty years later.

GOING HOLLYWOOD

Chicago White Sox star Ted Lyons (left) and manager Jimmy Dykes (center) pose for a Warner Bros. publicity shot with movie star Dennis Morgan, circa 1940. Dykes made his only known movie appearance in *The Stratton Story,* the film about real-life White Sox pitcher Monty Stratton, who lost a leg in a hunting accident in 1938 and then came back to pitch in the minors with a wooden leg for many more years. But that movie came out in 1949, an actor played Ted Lyons, and Dennis Morgan's name doesn't show up in the credits at all. So this photograph remains something of a mystery.

SMALL PARADE

Philadelphia Athletics manager Connie Mack (far left), star pitcher Eddie Plank (next to Mack), and others pose in California after the Athletics' 1913 World Series victory over the New York Giants. Note the lack of a cheering throng and the glum participants. It must have been very galling to Mack to see the champion A's get such little attention. And he had every right to be frustrated: Just a week later, John McGraw and his Giants would engage the Chicago White Sox in an exhibition game in Oxnard, California, that would see local schools shut down, attendance in the thousands, and national newspaper coverage.

#2191 Nov. 5th 1913   CONNIE MACK
                       EDDIE PLANK
                       W. JONES
                       H. HOLTZWORTH
                       C. EBERHART

CHAMPIONS

OAKLAND

ADVICE FROM A DEITY

Members of the Junior Red Devils cluster around Babe Ruth for some baseball tips. But Ruth never felt equipped to give advice to others. "All I can tell them is pick a good one and sock it," he said. "I get back to the dugout and they ask me what it was I hit and I tell them I don't know except it looked good." Still, even if his advice wasn't applicable to their own careers, do you think these boys minded? Each and every one of them undoubtedly remembered this meeting for the rest of their lives.

HERO WORSHIP

Just look at the expression on this young girl's face as she gazes up at Babe Ruth. In an age before television, before radio, the magnificent Ruth must have seemed as gigantic and mythical—as legendary—as Paul Bunyan even to children who never got the chance to see him play. To be down on the field with him, to stand beside him, to be on the receiving end of one his cockeyed grins, was a thrill of a lifetime. It certainly was for the girl pictured here, one Jean Farrington, who years later took the time to donate this treasured image to the National Baseball Hall of Fame Library.

ALOHA!

"Aloha" means hello *and* goodbye in Hawaiian, and that's exactly what Babe Ruth said to the baseball as he slugged a long one during this 1933 exhibition game in Honolulu. The Babe, as the *New York Times* commented, "hampered somewhat by white and yellow flower leis hung about his neck by enthusiastic Hawaiians, went through his entire repertoire before a capacity crowd of 15,000.... The Bambino played in the outfield and first base, took a turn in the pitcher's box, hit a home run and struck out." In other words, he gave the crowd everything they could have dreamed of.

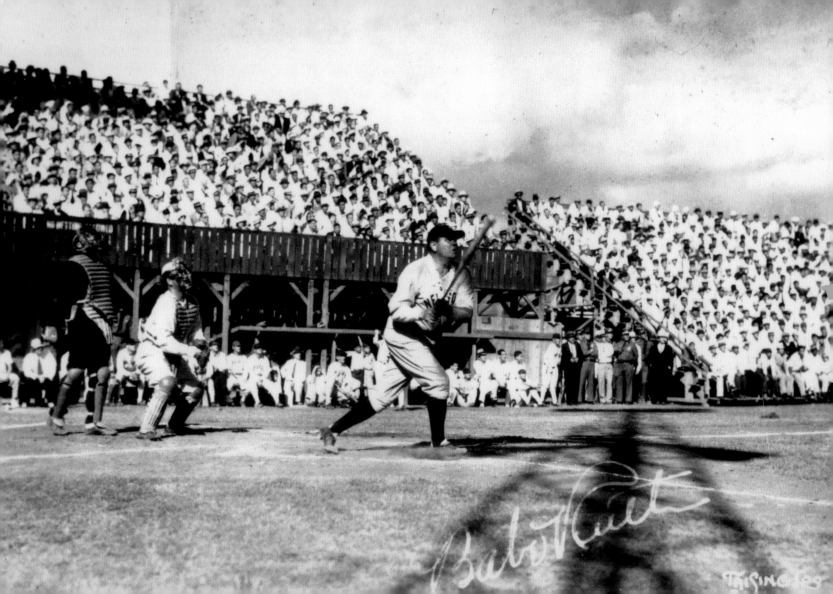

Babe Ruth

Prisinger

SANTA BABE

Babe Ruth entertains a tot at the Children's Tubercular Hospital in Seattle, Washington, in this undated photograph. It is remarkable how many photographs exist of Ruth with children—and how he and the kids always seem to be getting equal pleasure from the interaction. In *Kings of the Diamond*, Lee Allen and Tom Meany wrote of the Babe: "His visits to children in hospitals were not part of a public relations policy dreamed up by the management, but genuine evidence of his love for children and the memory of his own pathetic childhood. He did not seek publicity, but unconsciously generated it wherever he went."

CHILD STAR

Cleveland Indians pitching sensation Bob Feller back home with his little sister Marguerite in 1937. By this time, Feller was a phenomenon (his high school graduation was national news), and though he had pitched only fourteen times in 1936, everyone knew he was a superstar in the making. Everyone was right: Rapid Robert went on to notch 266 career victories, lead the league in strikeouts seven times, and march into the Hall of Fame. This photo reminds us that Feller was a mere child, just eighteen years old and fresh off an Iowa farm, when he stepped into the spotlight. Somehow he survived the pressures of fame—survived and thrived.

THE BABE'S BUNCH

Babe Ruth poses with children from an orphan home in 1926. (Note the Babe Ruth Home Run candy bars clutched in eager hands, and the chocolate-smeared faces.) "Ruth's subjects range from the articulate child in knickerbockers to his grandsire. Fill in with all ages, classes, and conditions of males, add the ladies who need to have baseball explained to them, and one has an idea of the empire of human hearts swayed by the specialist in home runs," opined the *New York Times* in an editorial entitled "The Baseball Hero." "If there be any who protest the space given by the newspapers to Ruth's prowess, let them consider how wholesome is the admiration he kindles."

THE QUIET MAN

Lou Gehrig acts as coxswain to a scullful of boys. By all accounts, the Iron Horse always enjoyed the time he spent with children. But unlike teammate Babe Ruth, the shy, introspective Gehrig rarely sought the spotlight. On the field and off, he always seemed to labor in the shadow of others. "Certainly he lacked the rumbling thunder and majestic presence of the Babe and the glint and glitter of Cobb; he seemed content to do the job well and let it go at that," wrote columnist Joe Williams.

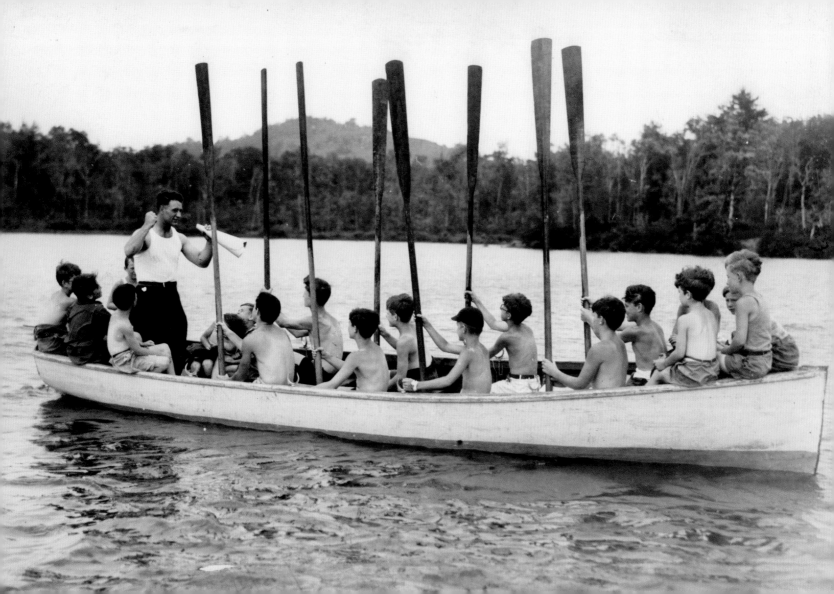

THE BABE AT PLAY

The countless photographs of Babe Ruth engaging in sports other than baseball make it clear that he threw himself into new tasks with great enthusiasm. He was always game for a new experience, whether it was wrestling or boxing or football, and always instantly recognizable, no matter what he was doing. "His round head, his button nose, his huge jowls, which obscured his square jaw, made Babe's face one in a million," Tom Meany wrote. "The broad shoulders and pipestem legs, the surprisingly thin arms and, in later years, the overhanging bay window, all were part of the Ruthian trademark."

CHAMP VS. CHAMP?

In the 1920s and 1930s, Babe Ruth and the peerless boxing champion Jack Dempsey came together every now and again. The two most famous names in sport during that era (and still two of the most famous today), they would pose in sparring position, the Babe laughing but looking a little apprehensive at being on the wrong end of Dempsey's lethal fists. The boxer facing Ruth in this obscure photograph is not identified, but the half-hidden profile certainly resembles Dempsey's. In any case, the circumstances surrounding the meeting—where it took place, the identity of the onlookers—have been lost to history.

SUPERSTAR SUMMIT

Commissioner Bowie Kuhn (second from left) looks on as Baltimore Orioles stars (left to right) Boog Powell, Frank Robinson, and Brooks Robinson exchange greetings with Japanese superstar Sadaharu Oh during a 1971 tour. Oh holds the worldwide career record for home runs with 868, but in eleven games against the Orioles during this 1971 visit, the great Japanese slugger went just six for fifty-four as the Orioles dominated the Giants. Overall in exhibition games against major-league teams, however, Oh did better, batting .260 in 338 at bats, with twenty-five home runs and a .524 slugging average—a power hitter's numbers indeed.

MPT

In 1909, his rookie year, Detroit Tigers shortstop Donie Bush (in back seat) was awarded this car after winning a contest as the most popular Tiger. (Ty Cobb led the A.L. with a .377 average, nine homers, and 107 RBI that season, but for some odd reason never did well in popularity contests.) Bush, though not a great player, later managed four major-league teams, owned and managed minor-league teams, and stuck around baseball for decades after his playing career ended in 1923. So why does he look so sour in this photo? Perhaps because his team-mates Sam Crawford (behind wheel) and Germany Schaefer won't let him drive his new car.

GET ME TO THE BALLPARK ON TIME

Hall of Fame outfielder Sam Crawford, presumably back in his hometown of Wahoo, Nebraska, during the 1905 off-season. Crawford, a lifetime .309 hitter in a nineteen-year career, was elected to the Hall of Fame in 1957, but memories of his play have faded. This may be because his career ended in 1917, just a couple of seasons before the advent of the lively ball, and because he fell just shy of amassing 3,000 career hits. Ty Cobb said that Crawford would have hit forty home runs a year during the Babe Ruth era. Instead, he holds the less-celebrated mark for most career triples: 312.

THE BEST WINTER-LEAGUE TEAM OF ALL TIME

Ladies and gentlemen, you are invited to marvel at the accumulation of talent that showed up during the off-season of 1954–55 to play for the Santurce Crabbers of the Puerto Rican winter league. Left to right, that's Willie Mays; Roberto Clemente; Buster Clarkson, a fine hitter who got only a cup of coffee in the majors after the color line was broken; Bob Thurman, a superb player who was also past his prime by the time he got his chance, but still was able to hit sixteen home runs in just 190 at bats with the Cincinnati Reds when he was forty; and George Crowe, who slugged thirty-one homers for the Reds in 1957. Needless to say, the Crabbers were a winter-league powerhouse in the 1950s.

THE TERMINATOR

On the flip side of the print of this photograph in the collection of the National Baseball Hall of Fame Library, someone has typed in "He'll be back." No, it's not a photo of Arnold Schwarzenegger, but of Willie Mays. The Say-Hey Kid is batting during the 1956 Hall of Fame game, just down the street from where they hang the plaques of the greatest ballplayers of all time. The twenty-five-year-old Mays had already banked seasons with forty-one and fifty-one home runs, 110 and 127 RBI, and .345 and .319 batting averages. His return to Cooperstown as a member of the Hall of Fame, already a certainty, took place in 1979.

NIXON'S THE ONE

Vice President Richard Nixon (second from left) boards a plane with Attorney General William Rogers, Washington Senators Roy Sievers (far left), and Harmon Killebrew (second from right) in 1959. Sievers ended his career with 318 home runs, Killebrew with 573 dingers and a reservation at the Hall of Fame. Rogers later led the investigation into the explosion of the space shuttle *Challenger*. But whatever became of Nixon?

CHAIRMAN OF THE BIG BOARD

Dapper in his Wall Street suit, Whitey Ford checks out the commodities market in 1959. In photographs like this one, Ford perfectly embodied the smooth, slick, corporate image of the Yankees in the 1950s, the seemingly clockwork way they seemed always to win while barely breaking a sweat. Between 1953 and 1964, Whitey chalked up double figures in wins every season as the Yankees cruised to ten A.L. pennants and five World Series championships. "Ford was the best clutch pitcher I ever saw and one of the smartest," said his teammate Mickey Mantle. Just not the most homespun.

BUCKY STYLE

Stanley Raymond "Bucky" Harris was a fine second baseman, but a so-so .274 hitter with no power during the lively ball era of the 1920s. His claim to fame was his managerial career—but even this was a bumpy road. In 1924, his first year as a manager, Harris led the Washington Senators to their first World Series championship. He helmed them to another pennant in 1925, but after that, in twenty-seven years as a manager, he finished first exactly once, with the 1947 Yankees, while ending up in fourth place or lower twenty-four times. His overall managerial record: 2,157–2,218. The life of even a baseball great can have more valleys than peaks.

THE CZAR AND THE CRAB

Judge Kenesaw Mountain Landis (left) seems to be looking for a way out of posing with Johnny Evers in this undated photograph from the 1920s. Though at first glance, the two men couldn't have been more different—Landis stoical, firm, dictatorial, and the mercurial Evers always seeming on the verge of jumping out of his skin with nervous energy—both shared a love of center stage.

GREAT CATCH!

Lou Gehrig celebrates landing a big one on a Jersey City fishing boat. It must have been a pleasure and a relief to Gehrig to get out of his uniform and do something just plain fun every once in a while. But he wasn't always so willing to have cameras present: Lou liked nothing more than to spend private time with his parents and, later, his wife, Eleanor. He was also a ballet fan, a fact he kept secret from the public throughout his career. Theaters would keep an aisle seat empty for him; Gehrig would enter after the lights went down and depart before the crowd rose—or noticed him—at the end of the performance.

GUESS WHO WON

Ty Cobb takes on all comers for an intense game of checkers during a 1919 visit to Ontario. Cobb did everything with the same fierceness and desire to win, an attitude you can see even in his posture and deduce from the expressions of his opponents in this photograph. No one ever knew when Cobb was going to lose his temper, take offense, or flare up. Al Stump, who knew Cobb well and helped him write his auto-biography, described Ty as the "most violent, successful, thoroughly maladjusted personality ever to pass across American sports," and that description was kinder than many.

About to make his play, Ty concentrates on a game of checkers at the Jack Miner Bird Sanctuary in Kingsville, Ontario — 1919.

STRIKE FORCE

Instead of counting sheep, perhaps sleepless ballplayers could have counted the battalions of umpires at this school for arbiters. Said ump Tim Hurst about his profession: "The pay is good, it keeps you out in the fresh air and sunshine, and you can't beat the hours." Of course, that was assuming you could ignore the howling fans, managers, and players.

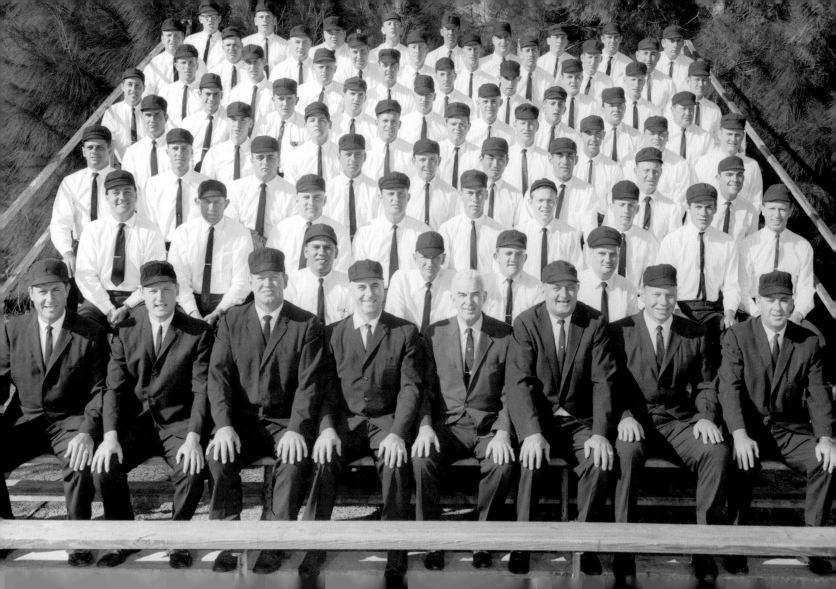

RETURN TO SENDER

After the conclusion of the 1888 season, sporting-goods magnate Albert Spalding, owner of the Chicago White Stockings (later the Cubs), took his team and an All-Star squad of opposing players off on a world tour. His goal was to spread the gospel—and also, presumably, to open up new markets for his products. The tour made stops in New Zealand, Australia, Ceylon, Italy, France, England, and (most famously) Egypt, where players posed beside the Sphinx and played before the great pyramids. Much to Spalding's disappointment, the game wasn't understood or enjoyed in many of the countries they visited.

Spalding American Base Ball Party. Chicago v.s. All Americas. (The Game at the Pyramids.) Feb. 9_1889.
P. Sebah (Cairo)

THE VISIONARY

John Montgomery "Monte" Ward (left), one of the leading figures of major-league baseball during its first fifty years, poses with three journalists assigned to cover the 1888–89 world tour pitting Cap Anson's Chicago White Stockings against Ward's All-Star team. Ward was a great player, a leading baseball writer, an unofficial member of the New York Giants' brain trust in the early twentieth century, and personal attorney to Giants manager John McGraw. He may be largely forgotten today, but Ward was as responsible as anyone for the growth of early baseball into America's pastime.

FAR FROM HOME

Writer, sporting-goods manufacturer, and team owner Albert Spalding described baseball as "the exponent of American Courage, Confidence, Combativeness; American Dash, Discipline, Determination; American Energy, Eagerness, Enthusiasm; American Pluck, Persistency, Performance; American Spirit, Sagacity, Success; American Vim, Vigor, Virility." Perhaps that's why those non-American countries visited by Spalding's 1888–89 world tour proved unexpectedly resistant to the game.

HIGH TIDE

Baseball had always been king in Washington, D.C. But by 1948, when this photograph was taken, there was a new contender for the throne: football, as demonstrated by this bizarre publicity photograph. The "pitcher" is Harry Gilmer, All-American halfback for the University of Alabama Crimson Tide football team, who had just begun his professional career as the number-one draft choice of the Washington Redskins. Gilmer played for the Redskins through 1954, but never achieved the stardom he'd garnered in college. At the time, no on could have predicted that football would soon become the chief obsession of the Capital's sports fans, or that baseball would soon disappear entirely from D.C. for more than thirty years before returning in 2005.

COME ONE, COME ALL

By 1916, when this game was played, Mordecai "Three Finger" Brown and Christy Mathewson had reached the end of their careers. (This would be the last major-league game for both.) But they were still enormously popular. During more than a decade, the two magnificent pitchers had faced off in a series of titanic battles as Brown's Chicago Cubs and Mathewson's New York Giants vied for supremacy in the National League. As the picture shows, Brown was missing parts of two fingers (lost in a childhood farm accident); as a result, his ball broke in unpredictable—and often unhittable—ways, which made him able to defeat even the great Mathewson.

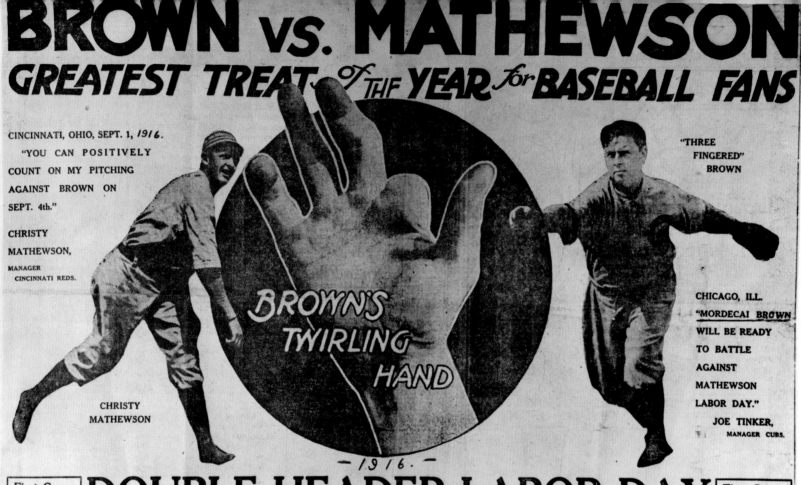

THE "OUT" GIRL

In the spring of 1931, Joe Engel, owner of the minor-league Chattanooga Lookouts (and baseball showman extraordinaire) signed a hard-throwing seventeen-year-old to a contract. What made the signing newsworthy was that the teenager was a girl: Jackie Mitchell, possessor of a wicked sinker. But Engel wasn't done. On April 2, 1931, he brought the New York Yankees into town for an exhibition game—and then summoned Mitchell to the mound. The petite righty proceeded to strike out Babe Ruth (who, in the words of an onlooker, "kicked the dirt, gave his bat a wild heave, and stomped back to the dugout") and a less demonstrative Lou Gehrig. Sadly, a few days later, Commissioner Landis banned women from professional baseball, calling it "too strenuous" for them.

A TRADITION THAT WILL LIVE FOREVER

"A Georgia Rebel Capitulates" read the headline that accompanied this photograph, released after Ty Cobb ended a holdout and signed with the Detroit Tigers in the spring of 1913. An unhappy-looking Tigers President Frank Navin makes sure Ty crosses all his T's. Holdouts were a common sight back in the "Golden Age" of baseball, as Cobb, Babe Ruth, Joe DiMaggio, and many other stars, denied free agency, battled for every penny they could get from the teams that owned them. Cobb, like most, gave good value: He hit .390 during the 1913 season.

BACK TO THE BALLPARK

The 1910 Chicago White Sox pose at Royal Gorge, Colorado, before their train continues its journey west towards the team's spring-training site in San Francisco. (That's future Hall of Famer Ed Walsh to the far right rear, brandishing a railroad flag.) After an off-season spent working in farms, stockyards, and factories, barnstorming, and getting reacquainted with their families, players were more than ready to begin a new pennant chase. And forget robins: For fans, the sight of players limbering up at the onset of spring training was the first real sign that the long, cold winter was over.

HOPE SPRINGS ETERNAL

Every new season brings its own fresh crop of hopeful rookies. Many never make it out of spring training, some go on to have substantial major-league careers, and a few earn a ticket to Cooperstown. This skinny rookie—this child—was one of the lucky few. It's eighteen-year-old Harmon Killebrew, circa 1954, trying to make the Washington Senators. Killebrew had to keep on trying: He played only a total of 113 games with the Senators during his first five seasons before finally establishing himself as an awesome power hitter and future Hall of Famer. But in the spring of the year, and of careers, happy endings like Killebrew's seem possible for every rookie.

THE FACE OF BASEBALL

The man posing patiently here is Charles Albert "Chief" Bender, superb pitcher with the Philadelphia Athletics during the early years of the twentieth century. By the time this photo was taken, Bender was forty years old and a coach with the White Sox. In his career, he'd matched breaking balls with Christy Mathewson and Cy Young; stared down Ty Cobb, Tris Speaker, and Tinker, Evers, and Chance; won his share of critical games and lost some, too. In other words, like every other player skilled and lucky enough to play in the majors, he'd become part of baseball's rich and endlessly surprising history.

Editor: Sharon AvRutick
Designer: Helene Silverman
Production Manager: Jane Searle

Library of Congress Cataloging-in-Publication Data

Wallace, Joseph E.
   Grand old game : 365 days of baseball / Joseph Wallace
        p.   cm.
   Includes bibliographical references and index.
   ISBN 13: 978-0-8109-5594-3
   ISBN 10: 0-8109-5594-6 (hardcover : alk. paper)
1 . Baseball—United States—Pictorial works. 2. Baseball—United States—Anecdotes.
I. Title.

GV867.4.W35 2004
796.357—dc22

                                        2004023455

Text copyright © 2004 Joseph Wallace
Illustrations copyright © 2004 National Baseball Hall of Fame and Museum

Printed and bound in China

10 9 8 7 6 5 4

HNA ▮▮▮▮▮▮
harry n. abrams, inc.
a subsidiary of La Martinière Groupe
115 West 18th Street
New York, NY 10011
www.hnabooks.com

FRONT COVER: Babe Ruth, still
   hustling, See May 17.
PAGE 3: Eddie Collins, dancing
   through his career. See July 1.
BACK COVER: Raising the flag on a
   new season. See February 28.